THE PISCO BOOK

Gregory Dicum AUTHOR

Shelley Alger PHOTOGRAPHER

Timothy Childs PRODUCER

Thomas Ingalls DESIGNER

ClearGrape LLC PUBLISHER

First Edition

©2011 Gregory Dicum and ClearGrape

Photographs ©2011 Shelley Alger unless otherwise noted

Published by ClearGrape LLC

200 California Ave, Bldg 180S

Treasure Island, San Francisco

California 94130

www.ClearGrapeLLC.com

ISBN: 978-0-615-42664-8

Library of Congress Control Number: 2011920931

Contents

Foreword 8

The First Sip 11

The Mists of Time 17

The Traditional Pisco-Making Process 27

The Golden Age of Pisco 41

Pisco Style and Pisco Culture 59

The New Generation and the Pisco Renaissance 69

Pisco Returns to America 93

Drinking and Recipes 105

Glossary 132
Index 134
Further Resources 136
Acknowledgements 137

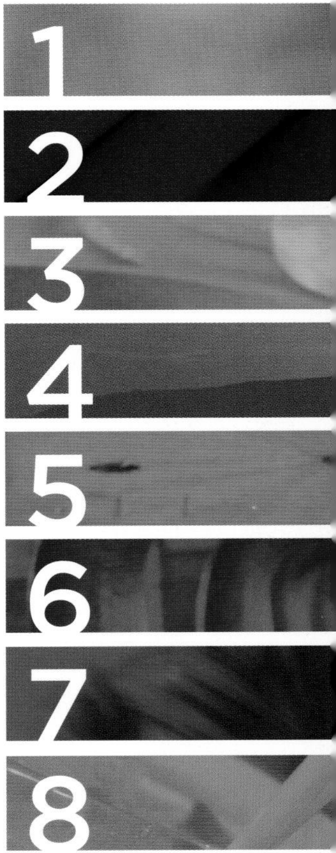

1
2
3
4
5
6
7
8

Foreword

Imagine you are on a quest to discover and develop great flavors and experiences. On your quest, you stumble upon an elixir that captures you, seduces you—even elevates you. And imagine that this engaging discovery is not only full of amazing flavors, it makes you feel great, is deeply rooted in history and is fun—from its elaborate preparation rituals to the people you meet along the way who share a passion for it. As you continue your exploration, you start to realize that you are just beginning to scratch the surface of an historical and inspirational fuel. Your curiosity is piqued. You must know more.

As you dive deeper into this world, you find many other "obsessives" who have dedicated part or all of their life's work to this magical stuff. At each turn, dip, and bend along this path, each discovery pulls you in further as you uncover how delightful and rich this nectar is—in substance as well as history.

That is what this book is about—it's about sharing the knowledge gained on a journey to understand and appreciate a magical elixir called pisco. Simply put, pisco is grapes converted into good wine, then distilled into a pure spirit; one of the purest spirits made.

As a serial entrepreneur, some of my talents lie in spotting and tracking (and sometimes building businesses around) emerging trends. I deeply believe in the future of pisco in America. No other spirit—by far—has such a compelling combination: a diverse flavor spectrum (based on grape varietal); spectacularly broad mixability (it mixes well in a very wide variety of cocktails); astounding purity (no flavorings or water; just grapes); inherent fruitiness (reduces the need for added sugar in cocktails); and, to boot, a unique 400 year old history. Many mixologists around the country are saying it's the most exciting new spirit to arrive on the scene since tequila. It's a whole new category—and I have absolutely no doubt it is about to become a barroom (and home shelf) staple.

Shelley and I created ClearGrape specifically to bring high quality pisco to an American audience. We began by importing a broad line of premium pisco from Bodega Viñas de Oro (known as ORO Pisco in the US)—to introduce the remarkable diversity of flavors available purely from different grape varietals. Our offerings extend with the development and launch of our own pisco brand this year, CODE, and we can't wait for you to try it.

We arrived at the idea for this book because we feel the American market for pisco is going to explode—yet very little information about this spirit is available in an accessible form. The book in your hands is the record of how we came to understand pisco—the spirit itself as well as the passionate people whose lives revolve around making it. It reveals the world of pisco as it was revealed to us on our early trips to Peru.

Our goal was to make a brand-neutral, fun, informative, and comprehensive guide that educates and delights. As pisco starts its US renaissance, we believe it's imperative for its success that all pisco brands in (or entering) the US work together to develop the pisco category as a whole, so that it takes its rightful place on bar and store shelves on par with tequila.

To entice you to begin experimenting with it, we've hand-selected and tested nearly 50 pisco cocktail recipes contributed by many top bar chefs/mixologists in the US and Peru. The online component of this book is waiting for you to explore even more new recipes and share your own (recipes, stories, and experiences). Please join the mix at www.thepiscobook.com.

Gregory Dicum turned out to be the perfect writer to accompany us on our journey to become experts. He has done a beautiful job chronicling the whole experience so we could share it with you. Shelley Alger (an accomplished travel photographer) skillfully documented our experience in the book's images. We hope The Pisco Book deepens your understanding, appreciation, and enjoyment of this magical spirit.

A special thanks to the team at Bodega Viñas de Oro for its time and energy in opening up the incredible world of Peruvian pisco to us. And to the many other talented souls who shared their experiences and knowledge with us, who helped make this book come to life: an immeasurable Thank You!

Cheers!

—Timothy Childs
San Francisco, 2011

The First Sip

Pisco is a mixable white spirit distilled from grapes, an elixir that has been made in Peru for 400 years. It is part of the Peruvian identity, the distilled essence of the coastal valleys south of Lima. It was named for the port of Pisco and still maintains its artisanal character. Today, pisco is undergoing a remarkable Renaissance; a sophisticated modern reinvigoration of something that goes all the way back to the origins of distillation at the hands of medieval alchemists. Yet for most people outside Peru, pisco is something completely new.

It's not often we get a chance to discover something so utterly genuine, so let's start from the beginning with the drink itself. Do you have a bottle of pisco (pronounced "PEES-ko") handy? Go ahead, pour yourself an ounce or so in a small stemmed glass—preferably a sherry glass or a cordial glass, if you have one.

Take a look: it's a crystal-clear liquor with a viscosity rare among white spirits. Take a sniff: it has a rich and heady aroma. Now take a sip: it's velvety and fruity, with a body that coats the tongue and infuses the palate with the varietal flavors of the grape.

Grapes? Varietals? Does it sound like we're talking about wine? In a way we are. Unlike almost every other distilled spirit, pisco is the straight distillate of fermented grape juice—wine, in other words. Grape spirits from elsewhere, like Italian grappa, are made from pomace, the skins and other solids left over from winemaking. Or, like cognac, they are distilled more than once, erasing their grape character into purified alcohol. Only French Armagnac is similar in that it is made from a single distillation of wine, but it is then aged in oak barrels that give it a dark color and distinctive flavor. Pisco, uniquely, is a clear spirit made from wine in a single distillation so that it maintains the varietal qualities of the grapes from which it was made. Defined narrowly, pisco is the essence of the grape and nothing more, a grape eau-de-vie.

And yet it is so much more. Like champagne or tequila, Peruvian pisco is an appellation. It is defined by a Denomination of Origin that stipulates the very specific conditions under which it must be made. Only eight grape varieties, which are grown in 42 coastal valleys in southern Peru, are permissible. The grape juice, or *mosto*, must be fermented with naturally occurring wild yeast, and it must be distilled using one of two specific kinds of copper pot stills. Pisco must emerge from the still at its final proof—between 38 percent and 48 percent alcohol, or around 80 proof—and nothing at all can be added, not even water. Finally, it must be stored in nonreactive vessels.

The process sounds deceptively simple, but it is more complicated than it seems. To start with, the eight grape varieties are divided into two groups: the so-called "aromatic" grapes, which contain high concentrations of fragrant, almost flowery compounds called terpenes in their skins, and "non-aromatic" grapes, which contain far lower levels. Each makes a distinctive *pisco puro*, or single-varietal pisco. The most common of these is pisco Quebranta, made from the Quebranta grape, a non-aromatic variety that evolved in Peru from Spanish vines. When different varietals are blended together, the result is a *pisco acholado.*

To further complicate matters, there are two styles of Peruvian pisco. Most pisco puro is made from mosto that has completed its fermentation; all the sugars have been converted into alcohol by the action of the wild yeast—in other words, young wine. But if the mosto is distilled while it is still "green," that is, before fermentation is complete, the result is a *pisco mosto verde*. Mosto verde is sweet, rich, and heady, with flavors that linger on the palate. Its body is so round and its flavors so complex, it is almost impossible to believe it is a white spirit.

Now is the ideal time to be discovering pisco. Though its history dates back to the Spanish conquest of Peru, by the late twentieth century it had fallen into a state of neglect, with poor production methods giving the drink a

bad name. In the past decade or so, a committed band of Peruvian grape growers, vintners, distillers, and marketers has, each in his or her own way, contributed to a resurgence in quality pisco. By combining modern technology with time-honored technique, they are producing some of the best pisco ever made. This Renaissance coincided with a rebirth of the classic art of mixology in the United States and Europe—perfect timing to restore pisco to its rightful place on the top shelf of bars around the world.

If you haven't tried it yet, you will soon. If you think you know it, it's time to take another taste.

That's what I did. I first tried pisco in 1989, on a trip to South America, and I can't say I sought it out on my return home. It would have been pointless anyway as there was simply no pisco to be had in the United States at the time. On subsequent trips to Peru, I drank a few obligatory pisco sours, but without much relish. Coming from a country that wows visitors with its incredible richness and diversity, the liquor didn't leave me with much of an impression.

I always love going to Peru, so I jumped at the chance to visit the pisco regions with photographer Shelley Alger and serial entrepreneur and tastemaker Timothy Childs in 2010. Fresh from Childs' success in creating TCHO, a new kind of chocolate company in San Francisco, the pair was starting a new venture — ClearGrape — to import Peruvian pisco to the United States. They invited me to come along to chronicle the story of pisco.

"Passion" is an overused word, but I challenge you to think of a better one to describe the inspired energy of the new generation of *pisqueros*, both in Peru and abroad. These people are driven: they obsess about vine roots, fermentation temperatures, specific gravity, and bottle design. They hunt for off flavors and mercilessly track them to their origins, forever in pursuit of the perfect sip. They never stop experimenting, pushing the boundaries of excellence for an appreciative—and growing—community of pisco connoisseurs around the world.

We visited bars, bodegas, vineyards, warehouses, workshops, and restaurants from Lima to Ica—the axis of the pisco region—talking to everyone we could. We gazed deeply into that glass of nectar, as though it were a crystal ball, and this book tells the story of what we saw.

— Gregory Dicum
San Francisco, 2011

OPPOSITE: Shelley Alger, Gregory Dicum, and Omar Cosio on the sand dunes outside Huacachina, near Ica.

The Mists of Time

Pisco is clear and elegant in the glass, but its history is murky, even disturbing. As any visitor to the pre-Columbian ruins that are literally everywhere in Peru knows, the modern country is the heir to a blood-soaked history.

When Spanish conquistadors led by Francisco Pizarro arrived in the Inca heartland in 1532, they lucked into what has to be one of the most brazen conquests of all time. Fewer than 200 Spaniards defeated an army of perhaps 80,000 natives that represented the most extensive empire in the Americas, a New-World Roman Empire.

Thanks to superior weaponry, the Spaniards killed some 7,000 Incas at their first encounter, and made a hostage of Atahualpa, their god-king. The conquerors demanded a room full of gold as ransom which the Incas, desperate to save their king, dutifully provided. The Spanish killed Atahualpa anyway.

This type of carnage did not arrive with the Europeans. The region's history is a story of constant strife. The Incas had just concluded a devastating civil war when the Spaniards arrived.

And in the aftermath of the conquest, different Spanish factions were at each other's throats (Pizarro himself was killed during this conflict) until Peru became a viceroyalty of the Spanish Empire in 1542.

The Spanish quickly acquired control over a fantastically wealthy empire that stretched from what is now northern Ecuador to southern Chile.

Modern-day Peru is the core of that empire. The country is so varied that different parts feel like different planets. The dry coast rises quickly to the Andes mountains, which reach the highest points in the Americas in the Cordillera Blanca, where snow-covered Huascarán soars to 22,205 feet. To the east, the Andes drop suddenly into the hot, humid flatlands of the Amazon Basin.

Francisco Pizarro

The country has seen countless civilizations rise and fall, with the Incas merely the last in millennia of indigenous cultures. As Ross Wehner, author of the guidebook *Moon Peru* told me just before my first trip there, "If you drive into any remote part of Peru, and stop the car and just start walking away from the road, I guarantee that you will find the re-mains of an undiscovered civilization." He knows because he's done it.

Many of the earliest peoples settled on the dry plain that runs the length of Peru's west coast, a desert comprising areas where a drop of rain has never been recorded. Yet rivers flow through the stark wilderness on their way to the Pacific from the lush Andes foothills, forming welcome ribbons of green in the desert. Like the Nile, which provided the conditions for the Ancient Egyptians to flourish, these rivers supplied the water and fertile land for highly developed civilizations to emerge.

Among them was the Nazca, an indigenous culture that emerged in the coastal desert region south of present-day Lima (the area that today produces the best pisco) more than 1500 years ago. They left behind the mysterious Nazca Lines on a plain outside the present-day city of Nazca. From the air, many of these lines, which are composed of rows of dark stones scraped off the lighter soil beneath, reveal themselves to be fantastic shapes—hummingbirds, spiders, marine life, and llamas that are hundreds of feet long.

THE SPANISH PLANT GRAPES

The rich valleys of the Ica region were equally attractive to the Spanish, who began to colonize the area 30 years after the conquest of the Incas. In 1563, Jerónimo Luis de Cabrera y Toledo, a conquistador, founded the city of Ica on the banks of the Ica River 160 miles south of Lima. In 1591, the Spaniards founded the town of Nazca near a cluster of pre-Columbian settlements. In 1640, they established a port at Pisco, which means "bird" in Quechua, an indigenous language spoken throughout the Americas (the rich marine ecosystem there is notable for its abundant bird life).

Part of the colonizing philosophy of the Spaniards was to attempt to re-create Iberian culture in new lands. This included the imposition of the Roman Catholic religion and the importation of Spanish-style agriculture, which centered on horses, cattle, wheat, olives, and wine.

Wheat and grapes, especially, were crucial as bread and wine are central components of the Catholic mass. The first wines in New Spain were carried there from the mother country and jealously guarded; at times clergymen, desperate to fulfill their sacred rites, were forced to beg for wine in Lima's plaza.

Grape vines were probably first planted in Peru in the 1550s. The Spanish discovered quickly that the dry air and plentiful water of the coastal valleys were ideally suited to grapes. By 1572, not a decade after the city was founded,

The Nazca Lines: A hummingbird 305 feet long.

Pisco is an *eau de vie* of grapes — the original distilled spirit.

Ica was producing 20,000 barrels of wine a year. By the 1620s, several chroniclers noted that Nazca, where wine-growers co-opted the traditional irrigation systems of the locals, was famous for producing excellent wine.

These wines were produced from grapes grown by natives, who were either forced to do so, often alongside slaves imported from Africa, or who grew vines on their own small plots of land. Experienced farmers indigenous to Nazca quickly learned the grape's ways and helped develop the distinctive *galera* system of viticulture, in which big vines are grown on a wooden "gallery" with the bunches of grapes hanging down so they can be harvested easily from below.

They also developed innovations in pressing grapes and drew upon longstanding and highly refined pre-Colombian ceramic techniques to make *botijas* (also called *piskos*) and *tinajas*—jugs and urns in which grape juice could be fermented into wine. One writer in 1623 estimated that half a million botijas a year were made in Ica, a time when the city was already famous in Spanish America for its wines. Similar abundance was springing forth to the south in Arequipa.

In fact, grape vines in Peru were too abundant. In the seventeenth century, in an effort to limit competition with Spanish wine in Spain and the Viceroyalty of Mexico, the Crown banned the export of wine from the Viceroyalty of Peru and attempted to limit the planting of grapes there. Yet in the 1620s, there was a big jump in production, and

by 1630 the Crown was paying for the Royal Navy at least in part through its wine tax in Peru. The tension between the mother country and the Ica winemakers persisted for centuries, with royal edicts frequently ignored, and Ica wine enjoyed in ports throughout the Spanish Americas.

It's possible that taxes on wine and the various rules controlling the trade stimulated the production of spirits, which were taxed differently. It is not known definitively when *aguardiente de uva*, or grape liquor, the drink that would later be called pisco, was first produced in the New World. The earliest written evidence is a will dated 1613 in which Pedro Manuel of Ica, known as "the Greek," left his possessions to the slave Isabel de Acosta. These included liquor in bottles, tinajas, and barrels as well as, most significantly, a copper still.

In the seventeenth century, distillation was widely practiced in Europe, so it is no surprise that it had made its way to the New World by then. Near Eastern alchemists first invented the process to separate the various components of liquid mixtures. It was later found that the distillation of fermented beverages resulted in concentrated alcohols (the word "alcohol" means "finely divided" in Arabic).

Clearly, the Greek's will indicated that at least one commercial distillery was in operation in Ica by around 1600, and there were undoubtedly more. By 1617 enough aguardiente de uva was being produced that a tax on liquor

OPPOSITE: Botijas at the Tabernero Bodega in Chincha. Dating back millennia, this style of clay pisco storage container is today almost entirely decorative.

was considered in Ica, and by 1630 grape liquor from Peru was known in Spain.

By 1704 records indicate that almost 50,000 botijas of grape liquor were exported from Callao, Lima's port, compared with only 35,000 botijas of wine. More than half went to Panama, then as now the main trans-shipment point to the Atlantic, suggesting that Ica grape liquor was known throughout the Spanish world.

MAKING AGUARDIENTE DE UVA

By then pisco-making had taken on the form that would remain largely unchanged for the next three centuries. Grapes were harvested by hand and brought to the *bodegas* (wineries), which were often on well-run Jesuit haciendas. There they were heaped into big vats and stomped. A further extraction of juice was accomplished using presses that employed the weight of huge *huarango* logs to bear down on the grapes. The huarango, a massive, long-lived desert tree with incredibly hard, dense wood, was the only timber native to the area; it was used for everything from fine furniture to firewood. Today, it is endangered and its cutting is prohibited, but big old trunks can still be found at bodegas around Ica.

After pressing, the grape juice, or *mosto*, was placed in waterproof tar-lined botijas or tinajas, where natural yeast from the grape skins caused it to ferment. Mosto literally

means "must," although in Peru it has a slightly different meaning than it does among American winemakers: mosto refers to the juice of the grapes, without seeds or skins, right up through fermentation.

After up to 60 days, the fermented wine was poured into the belly of a copper still—either a *falca*, a simple pot with a long tube running down from its lid, or an *alembique*, a more advanced design with a "swan's neck" on top. The still was heated over a fire of huarango wood so that the heated vapors of alcohol and other compounds rose in the still and proceeded into a coiled copper tube immersed in a bath of cool water. There, the vapors would condense and travel to the end of the pipe, outside the tank.

After the "head"—the first distillates, which are toxic compounds like methyl alcohol—the liquor turns and runs crystal clear. This "body" was then collected and stored in botijas, ready to be sent around the Spanish world.

PISCO IN THE VICEROYALTY OF PERU

In the seventeenth century, production of aguardiente de uva was centered on Pisco, Ica, and Nazca in the north, and Arequipa and Moquegua in the south. Wine and liquor from the southern region supplied the highlands stretching from Cuzco into what is now Bolivia. Once the Inca heartland, this important region was the source of Spanish silver, which was critical to its economy. Spaniards working in the mines favored grape liquor, leaving wine for the natives and African slaves, of whom there were millions over the centuries, living short, miserable lives in dangerous, inhospitable conditions. The liquor was transported in caravans of mules, donkeys, and llamas, a botija or leather flask slung on either side of each beast, just as the Incas had done. The round-trip took two or three months.

The northern aguardiente de uva producers, meanwhile, supplied Lima and, through the port of Pisco especially, the burgeoning export market. It was because foreigners associated aguardiente de uva with the port of Pisco that the beverage acquired that name. The oldest-known foreign reference to Peruvian aguardiente de uva as "pisco" was published in 1825, but the term was likely in use long before.

By the nineteenth century pisco had its own two-century-long history in Peru, complete with indigenous grape varieties. Most of the grapes originally brought to Peru by the Spaniards had come from vineyards in the Canary Islands. Still a part of Spain today, this archipelago off the coast of Africa is perfectly positioned as a stopover point for ships traveling between Spain and the Americas. At the time, the Canary Islands produced wine for export to England, using grapes derived from Spanish stock.

The first grapes brought to the New World were hardy black grapes like the Negra Corriente or Negra Criollo vari-

ety, known as Mission Black in California, where they were also introduced by the Spaniards. Negra Corriente remains one of the grapes used in making pisco today.

At some point, probably in the eighteenth century, a mutation of Negra Corriente was discovered in Ica. It was given the name Quebranta, meaning "broken", and it quickly became the dominant pisco grape, a distinction it still holds today.

From early on, *pisco puro*—that is, pisco made from a single varietal—and *pisco acholado* were both widely produced. The latter may be made from different grapes pressed together, different mostos mixed together, or different pisco puros mixed after distillation. It is known as "pisco acholado," or blended pisco, because it was made by "cholos," workers of mixed indigenous and Spanish ancestry, from the mixed grapes left over by the landowners. As happens so often with pisco, there is also an alternate story: acholado may be so-called because it is a mix of grapes, the way cholos were a mix of ancestries. Perhaps both have an element of truth.

The history of pisco is filled with periods of abundance alternating with serious setbacks. In the early 1600s a series of huge earthquakes and volcanic eruptions around Arequipa cut the region off from Lima and destroyed many of its large bodegas. In 1767, as a result of competitive tension between the Jesuits and the Spanish Crown, the Jesuits were expelled from the Spanish Empire and their wealth was largely appropriated by the state. The Franciscans replaced the Jesuits, but their lack of commercial prowess sent pisco production—and quality—into a tailspin.

But the worst setback for pisco came with Peruvian independence from Spain. In 1807, when Napoleon's Grande Armée invaded Spain, the New World viceroyalties were suddenly cut off from the rest of the Spanish Empire. This power vacuum allowed different local interests in South America to assert themselves, initiating a period of conflict that lasted from 1809 until the Peruvian Declaration of Independence in 1821—years of chaos that interrupted the production and export of pisco, and even sometimes resulted in the destruction of valuable stores of the liquor at the hands (and livers) of marauding armies.

OPPOSITE: A lilliputian working prototype of a copper alembique.

Dusty Vines, Clay Jugs, and Battered Copper
The Traditional Pisco-Making Process

Outside the city of Ica, the Ica Valley stretches north and south, hemmed by black, stony mountains to the east and fields of huge, starkly beautiful sand dunes to the west. This looming, inhospitable wilderness would seem terrifying but that the valley itself is a rich, green agricultural cornucopia. Flat and ideally suited to cultivation, it is a patchwork of fields of asparagus, pecan and avocado groves, and vineyards.

Through the middle, the paved Pan-American Highway serves as the valley's main thoroughfare. The world's longest drivable road, it stretches from the southern tip of South America to the Arctic Ocean in Alaska with just a single tough spot in Panama. In the Ica Valley dusty byways, bordered by eucalyptus windbreaks, head off the road into the fields. Here and there small villages of dust-covered adobe houses crowd the roadside.

North of Ica, one of these little roads leads to the hacienda owned by Rodolfo Mejía. At 83 years old, he's known as "La Leyenda"—the Legend—by the region's pisco-makers. "I've made pisco since 1940," he told me when I visited, "in this same place, one of the oldest bodegas in Ica."

The bodega certainly looks old, partly because it is, and partly because it is still suffering damage from the devastating 2007 earthquake that flattened much of Pisco and ruined buildings throughout Ica. Among the losses at La Leyenda's hacienda was the huge brick kiln for firing botijas, one of only two left in the country. It's now a caved-in pile of dust-colored bricks, a great archaeological loss, even though it hadn't been used in more than a century. A few small bodegas like Mejía's still ferment their mosto in botijas but the jars are all valuable antiques now, and every year there are fewer, victims of time and, as we shall see, progress.

But at Bodega Mejía, progress hasn't been an issue. "We are making pisco the same as ever," said La Leyenda. "Over there we have the huarango press. We have it all." I followed his gaze from the shady porch, across the sun-baked courtyard, to the pisco-making equipment near the gate. And there it was: a classic old huarango press, it consisted of a huge, old forked trunk of the hard, heavy wood held aloft by a big, hand-carved screw, also made of huarango wood. Attached to the log at one end was a circular wooden panel, like a big wagon wheel, and I could see that by turning the screw, the panel would be lowered into the concrete tank beneath it.

Next to that tank was the primary tank, where fresh grapes are piled up during *La Vendímia* (the harvest) for stomping. The stompers work all through the night, the better to avoid the yellow jackets, which are as enthusiastic about the harvest as the pisco-makers themselves. Several abreast, arms linked, the stompers methodically reduce the pile of grapes into a slurry, with the liquid part—the mosto—draining into other tanks.

In modern production the mosto may be macerated with the skins for up to 48 hours, thus developing further varietal character in the finished product, although in the past some superfine pisco was made with grapes carefully peeled by hand, one of the many benefits of available slave labor.

The pomace, the solid mass of skins and stems, is placed into the tank beneath the huarango log, and the wooden panel is lowered onto it, bringing thousands of pounds of weight to bear. More mosto is extracted in this way, and the remaining solid cake of skins and stems—the *queso*, or cheese—is discarded.

Bodega Mejía still ferments some of its mosto in botijas, three-foot-tall tar- or wax-lined earthenware jugs sealed with a mud mixture. Also known as *piskos*, they are shaped in the traditional indigenous style with pointy bottoms like Roman amphorae (but without the handles). They are carefully stacked leaning against one another in the sun during fermentation.

Though his bodega is in disarray, La Leyenda is not. He dresses sharply in khaki pants and jacket that match

the tan soil of his hacienda. Even his lined face, after eight decades in the Ica sun, has taken on the color of the soil. But his blue eyes remain clear and penetrating behind his wire-rimmed glasses.

LAS ONCE AT BODEGA MEJÍA

After we had been talking a while, La Leyenda got up and disappeared into the darkness of his house, from where we could hear classical music playing, echoing lightly off cool blue tiles. He came back with a glass jug filled with crystal-clear pisco and a single glass—a *mulita*, or shot glass.

In the old Ica style, we all shared the glass. "Let me drink first," said don Mejía, "it's traditional for the host to drink first, to show it's not poisoned. *¡Salud!*"

And with that, he downed a hearty shot, the customary four fingers of *las once*, the 11:00 a.m. tipple. He filled the mulita again and passed it to me.

"*¡Salud!*" I said, looking him in the eye, and knocked it back.

La Leyenda saw the look on my face. "It's strong!" he said, "*¡Pisco macho!* I keep it at 45 percent—a higher strength means fewer impurities!"

It was an acholado, a blend of Quebranta and Moscatel, with a good, smoky farmhouse flavor to it—and it was potent. By the time the mulita had made the rounds of everyone present, the conversation was animated, jumping from the lime tree in front of the house (the traditional morning draught is nothing but lime and pisco) to mosto verde, pisco made from incompletely fermented wine ("It's only for the rich," according to La Leyenda, "a whim of millionaires") to Chilean pisco ("It's not pisco!").

A tall, ornate wooden cross stood in the courtyard by the entrance to the bodega. It was decorated with the tools of the pisco-making trade: grape-harvesting equipment, a ladder, and pruning shears. The cross was topped with a portrait of Jesus, and its arms held the sun and the moon. At its base were some sinister-looking items: a skull and crossbones, and a trio of dice. I noticed other wooden crosses covered in faded cut paper hanging above the still.

These talismans are traditional accoutrements of pisco-making, which has, over the centuries, acquired many customs that pisco-makers ignore at their peril: nobody would dream of running the still without a little prayer, perhaps an offering of pisco to the ground, and a protective flower-garlanded cross above the spigot that presents the distiller with the fresh liquor.

The copper still is the heart of the pisco-making operation. At Bodega Mejía it was dark with age, a little battered, and surrounded by earthquake rubble, but not too far from La Leyenda's operation, we saw some brand-new examples of this ancient technology.

MAKING ALEMBIQUES

Jesús Amoretti Yataco has been making copper stills by hand at his workshop in Chincha, north of Pisco, for his entire life. He learned the trade from his father, who learned from his grandfather, an immigrant who brought the craft with him from Italy more than a century ago. Today, don Amoretti is teaching his sons.

They work together in an open-air shed behind their modest unpainted brick house. The yard is strewn with tools, copper piping, and sheets of copper. Above the seeming disorder, a big, beautiful still sits gleaming like an apparition.

It is an alembique, one of the two types of stills allowed for pisco-making, and the only kind still manufactured. It consists of a big, flat-bottomed copper vessel ("This one can hold 400 liters," don Amoretti says, slapping it lovingly) topped by a smaller bulb that in turn leads into an elegantly swooping swan's neck.

When fermented mosto is placed in the alembique's belly and it is heated from below (traditionally using huarango wood, but now most often with natural gas), the volatile compounds in the mosto, including ethanol, evaporate and pass into the swan's neck. This copper tunnel narrows downwards into a coiled copper tube held away from the

Pisco is made in copper stills, like the earliest distilled alcohols of nearly a millennium ago.

OPPOSITE:
top: Jesús Amoretti Yataco; *center*: don Amoretti's granddaughter; *bottom*: don Amoretti and his son in front of a "semicontinuous" alembique.

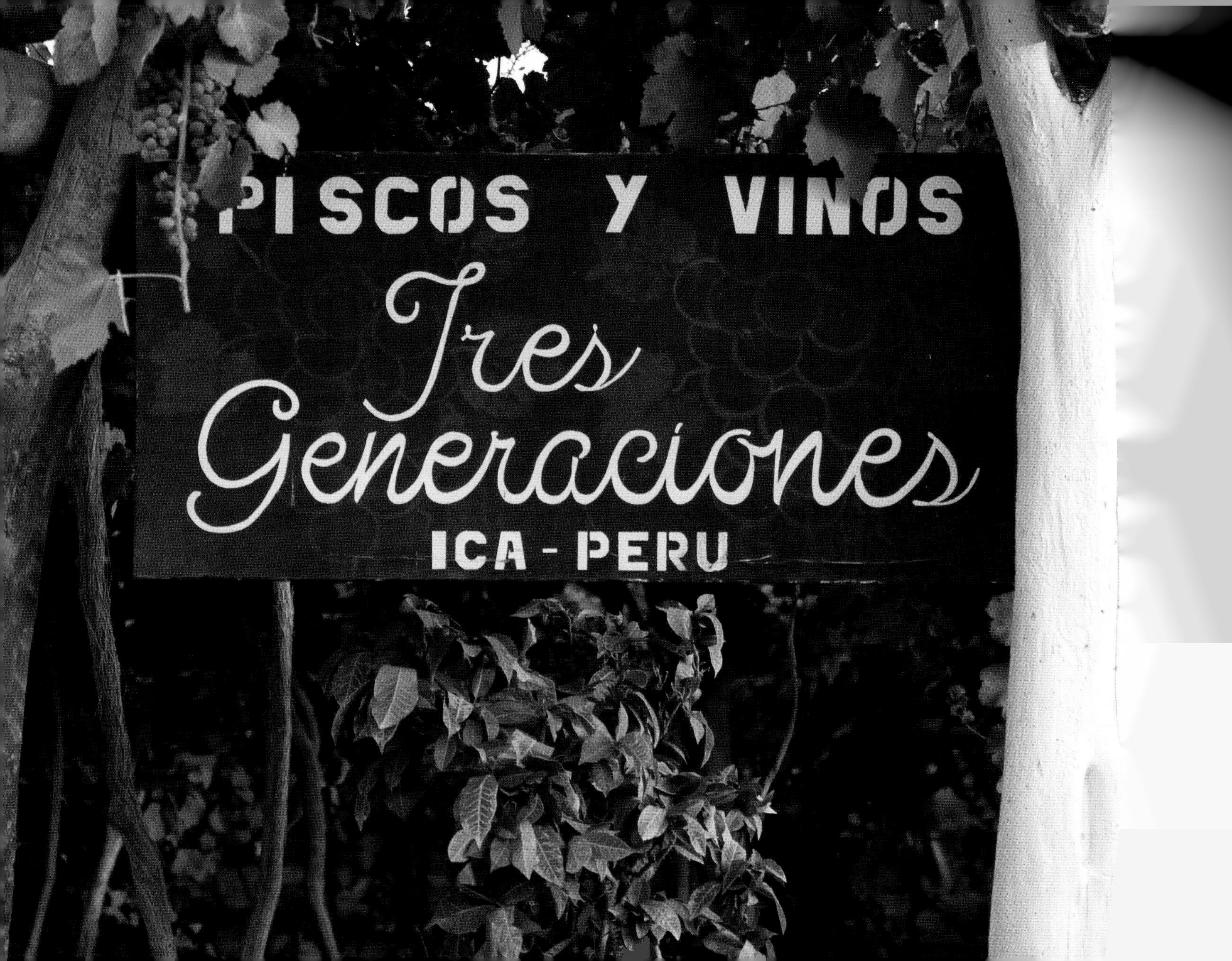
PISCOS Y VINOS
Tres
Generaciones
ICA - PERU

body of the still. In operation, the coil is submerged in water to aid in the cooling and condensation of the liquor.

"This one is semi-continuous," don Amoretti told me, pointing at another copper vessel connected to the still's belly, which he called a *calientevino*, or wine-heater. The tube from the swan's neck disappeared into this pre-heater. Inside, another coil filled the container. In operation, this device pre-heats the next batch of mosto, while also cooling the distillate somewhat. When it is time to change batches, the next batch is already hot and less energy is needed to begin the distillation process. (True continuous stills, in which the unit does not have to be stopped between batches, are used for industrial-scale production of many kinds of alcohol but are not permitted for pisco.)

Don Amoretti makes everything by hand with lead-free bronze solder and copper rivets. The only concession to modernity is a pneumatic hammer that allows the team to shape copper more quickly than with a handheld hammer. Even so, making an alembique is a careful, artisanal process. "It takes 30 days to make a small one like this," said don Amoretti, indicating the 400-liter alembique. "An alembique of a thousand or 1200 liters takes two and a half months, three months if it has a calientevino."

Thanks to recent increases in the price of copper, it now costs $22,000 to purchase one of don Amoretti's thousand-liter alembiques. He has made more than 150 of them in his career.

"Alembiques my father and grandfather made are still in service," he told me, "I've repaired a few of them. They made them with really thick copper. They can last a century. We use a lot thinner copper—only a few big companies can afford the thick copper now—but even so, these will last 40 or 50 years."

Don Amoretti explains that the age of an alembique does not affect the flavor of the pisco it produces—more important is its size. "The mosto boils for too long in the big ones," he told me. "It cooks for eight or ten hours and the pisco has a burnt quality. In the smaller ones it's only on the fire for a couple of hours, and the quality of the pisco is better. Four or five hundred liters is the best."

TRES GENERACIONES

Back in Ica, not far from the Bodega Mejía, is Tres Generaciones, a bodega run by Juanita Martínez de Gonzales and her husband Luís António Gonzales Martínez. Doña Juanita, especially, is beloved in the Ica Valley for her dedication to marrying the best of the old ways with contemporary efficiencies.

Tres Generaciones is one of several bodegas clustered together on the road leading to the Mejía place. Don Antonio's family has operated it since the 1850s, but doña Juanita has been the force behind its modernization into a highly respected brand of top-quality pisco in Peru.

The road leading to the bodega is tightly hemmed by tall, whitewashed walls. The surface of the road is covered in dried pomace left over from pressing the grapes, a traditional way of keeping the dust down which gives the dry air a light scent of raisins. The bodega itself is orderly and spotlessly clean, all concrete, brick, and rows of well-tended grapes. To the rear, a pecan orchard provides much-needed shade.

In front Tres Generaciones runs a popular open-air restaurant where visitors can try traditional pisco drinks and Iqueño cuisine. Bodega tours have become a big draw as tourism in Peru grows, and the efficiently casual restaurant at Tres Generaciones is no doubt a large part of doña Juanita's strategy—she says it's responsible for half her profits.

But the heart of her operations is in the rear, under the shade of the pecan orchard next door. There, doña Juanita distills and matures her pisco. Until 2007 Tres Generaciones did not even use alembiques, preferring instead the older, simpler *falca* design for their stills.

Unlike alembiques, falcas have a simple chamber that leads directly into a long, straight copper tube at the top, called a "cannon." It certainly resembles one, jutting straight out of the falca's lid before it narrows and joins with a copper coil just like the ones found on alembiques.

The design of the falca is ancient; it is reminiscent of the first stills used by the alchemists of old—nothing but a chamber for heating the mosto and a tube for collecting the distillate. In the earliest Spanish colonial days, when copper still parts were being brought from Spain, it was the most efficient design for transporting: the copper parts consist only of the cannon, the lid, the coil, and the *paila*, or pan, at the bottom. The sides of the falca are not metal at all; rather it is a brick or concrete chamber lined with a special cement that includes egg whites and sugar.

"The age of the copper does not matter, but the age of the paila is important," doña Juanita told me as we stood above the falca. Hers is more than 120 years old. "Ours was one of the first pailas to come to Ica. The old pailas, especially those made for people who had a lot of money, contained a percentage of gold in the copper, to create a better quality of pisco. We have a little in this one."

I stuck my head inside to take a look—the paila gleamed copper beneath me. "You can't see it," doña Juanita said from behind me, her voice echoing inside the 1700-liter falca. Though she is physically tiny, she has a big, generous personality that seemed to naturally fill the cavernous still. "But you can taste it—it gives a great pisco."

In 2007 when she wanted to expand this traditional style of production, doña Juanita discovered that nobody makes falcas anymore—like botijas, they are living antiques. Reluctantly, but with the encouragement of her son,

OPPOSITE: Juanita Martínez de Gonzales, left, showing Gregory Dicum, Timothy Childs, and Omar Cosio the secrets deep inside the falca at Tres Generaciones.

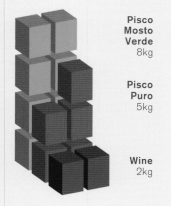

Volume of Grapes Needed to Make One Liter

Pisco Mosto Verde
8kg

Pisco Puro
5kg

Wine
2kg

Image source: ClearGrape LLC

Luís António Gonzales Martínez, with whom she undertakes the day-to-day operation of Tres Generaciones, she bought an alembique. Now she runs the two side by side, and has become an expert on the differences between them.

According to doña Juanita, pisco from an alembique has cleaner aromas because the alembique does a better job of removing impurities (including agricultural chemicals) from the distillate, and provides a better yield. But the falca, if run carefully, makes a pisco with more body.

In essence, the falca accentuates both the good and the bad in the mosto, making it a riskier still for any but the surest pisco-makers. No strangers to careful pisco-making, Tres Generaciones uses their falca to make piscos with aromatic grapes and the alembique for the non-aromatics. They also make a few piscos that are blends of distillate from the two stills. "The mix creates an excellent pisco," says doña Juanita, "with both body and aroma."

The swan's neck that tops an alembique serves as a primitive retort that purifies the vapors somewhat: heavier compounds condense inside it and drip back into the pot while lighter constituents of the vapors pass on into the coil. It is the same principal that, taken to the extreme in a rectifying column, lets producers of other kinds of liquors achieve very high proofs of nearly pure alcohol that they then "rectify," or dilute with water. That's not something you want in pisco.

"You have to conserve the aromas," points out doña Juanita, "that is what is distinctive about each grape. Quebranta doesn't have much aroma, but the falca conserves it—in the alembique you lose it."

Doña Juanita prizes the varietal flavors of the grapes in her pisco, and in this she is decidedly modern. Her pisco is very different from don Mejía's. "The piscos of the old days were well made," she says, "except that they had an excessive level of alcohol—they were *piscos de los machos*, with 50 percent alcohol." Hers are around 40 percent alcohol (the allowable range today is 38 percent to 48 percent).

She also differs from don Mejía in that she makes mosto verde, which is simply pisco made from grape juice that has been incompletely fermented. This means that the mosto contains unfermented sugars, and thus less alcohol. In the still, this combination leads to a richer, more aromatic pisco, but at a price: pisco-making is a process of distilling the essence of the grape, so mosto verde has a much higher grape intensity than ordinary pisco. It might take two kilos of grapes to make a bottle of wine, while it takes five kilos to make a bottle of pisco puro. A bottle of pisco mosto verde can contain the distilled essence of a whopping eight kilos of grapes.

Modern pisco-makers closely monitor the fermentation of their mosto, for once alcoholic fermentation is complete, malolactic conversion begins. While this is an important part of winemaking, it leads to a terrible off flavor in pisco known as "baby's vomit."

Mosto fully ferments in about 14 days, depending on its temperature. Many people make pisco mosto verde from mosto that has fermented for just 72 hours or less. In the old days, when the Jesuits let their mosto ferment for 60 days, the difference between ordinary pisco, with its foul malolactic tinge, and sweet, smooth mosto verde must have been even more dramatic than it is today—something for the millionaire's table indeed.

Tres Generaciones still uses wood fires to heat their stills. Traditionally, the hot coals provided by the heavy huarango wood were preferred, but that is illegal today. "The temperature of the fire is really important," says doña Juanita, "you have to control it carefully; you don't want the pisco to come out too quickly. It's the same as cooking. For me, the most exquisite food is that cooked over firewood."

A stickler for time-honored ways, doña Juanita is successful because she is also open to advances when they meet her conservative standards for what ends up in the

FALCA

1 Heat Source
2 Mosto
3 Condensation of alcoholic vapors
4 Cooling vat
5 Pisco (Aguardiente)

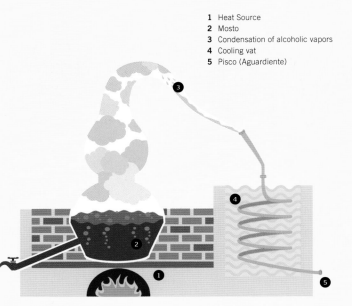

ALEMBIQUE

glass. "Now that we have an alembique," she admits, "we like it."

In other areas, like the aging of her piscos, she has been even bolder. Even with a careful separation of head, body, and tail, the pisco that comes directly out of the still is harsh, with many strong volatile components. It is called *chicharrón* at this stage, and must undergo a few months of *reposo*, or rest, in order to mellow. To retain its clear color, pisco must be aged in nonreactive containers. Customarily, this meant tar-lined tinajas or barrels.

Tres Generaciones used to employ barrels lined with paraffin, but once they lost their supply of the good English stuff, they started to notice off flavors after resting. So they looked at the modern options: stainless steel and food-grade plastic. Surprisingly, doña Juanita chose the plastic. "It's warmer than steel," she says.

We were sitting under a Quebranta trellis, shaded by the spreading green leaves, with the young grapes just forming above, nothing more than tiny green berries. We were enjoying doña Juanita's mosto verde Quebranta, which reminded me of the sun itself, when she brought out something so rare most pisco aficionados have never tried it—a six-year-old mosto verde Quebranta.

It was incredibly smooth, with the mouthfeel of an aged whiskey but the complete absence of color typical of Peruvian pisco. It was nothing but clean, buttery flavors, with some melon and a hint of citrus—an exceptional pisco by any measure. Only 10 percent of Tres Generaciones' annual production of 50,000 liters goes into long-term aging like this—including aromatics and some boutique piscos—but none of it has been released to the market. Yet.

It was the ideal marriage of tradition and technology, brought together by a critical third ingredient. "A good producer has a lot of passion for the things they are doing," doña Juanita said, holding a glass of her beautiful pisco aloft, so we could see the dusty leaves of the Quebranta vine through it. "You can't be satisfied until things are the way you want them."

OPPOSITE: Omar Cosio, Timothy Childs, Gregory Dicum, Juanita Martínez de Gonzales and her son, Luis Antonio Gonzales Martínez, toasting under the Quebranta trellis with a five year old pisco Italia.

Chilcanos, Punches, and Sours
The Golden Age of Pisco

In some ways, independence from Spain was the beginning of Peru's problems. In place of more than two centuries of relative calm, paid for by oppression and economic exploitation, in 1821 independent Peru—like much of independent South America—was at the dawn of a period of political chaos. In its first 60 years, 49 different men served as president, 10 of them put in office through coups. On three different occasions, multiple people claimed to be president. Throughout this confusion, they presided, if that is the word, over bleak economic stagnation.

Even though pisco acreage never again reached the extent of its heyday in the eighteenth century, producers found new export markets in the next century. The end of the Viceroyalty and increasing American and British commercial power in South America brought more foreign visitors to Peru, many of whom took a great interest in pisco.

In 1825 William Bennet Stevenson, a British merchant and adventurer who spent twenty years in South America (he wound up in the Chilean navy), became the first known foreigner to write of aguardiente de uva as "pisco." Among other details, he reported that together the lands

THE CHINCHA (GUANO) ISLANDS: MIDDLE ISLAND, AS SEEN FROM NORTH ISLAND.

The Chincha (Guano) Islands from The Illustrated London News, 21 February 1863.

around Pisco (which he described as a "miserable village"), Chincha, and Cañete produced 150,000 gallons of pisco each year, and described the process, noting that the stills in use were archaic even by the standards of the day.

In 1829 British reverend Hugh Salvin wrote of his 1824 visit to Pisco, "The district is celebrated for the manufacture of a strong spirit, called after the name of the town." He also recounted that the monks very much enjoyed their pisco, and that there were different grades of the drink.

Johann Jakob von Tschudi, a Swiss doctor, was another traveler who wrote of his visit to Peru from 1838 to 1842. But unlike the others he ventured inland from Pisco to Ica (which he called Yca). Von Tschudi chronicled "Yca brandy" and its importance to the region: "Scarcely anything but the vine is cultivated in the Haciendas of the environs; and this branch of husbandry contributes greatly to enrich the province."

He also described a landscape very similar to today's. "It is astonishing to see with what facility the vine thrives in a soil apparently so unfruitful..." he wrote. "Whilst the surrounding country bears the appearance of a desert, the vineyards of Yca are clothed in a delightful verdure."

Although pisco merited a mention by these early authors, all of them considered the local guano production to be more important. The huge deposits of this nitrogen-rich seabird dung on the small islands just off the coast were an ideal fertilizer. Guano had been exploited both by the Incas (the name "guano" derived from a Quechua word) and the Spaniards, especially the Jesuits who used it for their vines. By the nineteenth century, it was the most significant commodity export from the area, fertilizing fields in North America and Europe.

When they did turn their attention to pisco, all three authors noted that the best pisco was called "Italia," and was made from grapes of the Moscatel family—an indication that the older, non-aromatic grape varietals had by then been joined by the aromatics, grapes with far higher terpene levels in their skins and concomitantly stronger floral aromas.

It is not entirely clear when the aromatic grapes arrived in Peru. One account from the mid-eighteenth century tells of "Italian" grapes grown in Lima, but for eating, rather than pisco-making. Others hold that the aromatics arrived shortly after independence, brought by Italian immigrants.

At any rate, it is clear that by the mid-nineteenth century, pisco made from Italia grapes was widely regarded as the best type. It is most likely that this high-grade pisco was mosto verde: in the absence of careful fermentation controls, the best way to avoid the "baby-vomit" defect is to distill the mosto before fermentation is complete. So, the top-grade exported pisco in this era was probably what is called *mosto verde de Italia* today.

THE WAR OF THE PACIFIC

Between guano and pisco, the region flourished after independence, even if the rest of Peru did not. Lingering territorial clashes among the new South American states did not help the political situation. In 1879 the War of the Pacific erupted between Peru and Bolivia on one side and Chile on the other. The basis of the conflict was disputed territories along the desert coast that happened to contain huge deposits of nitrates—natural mineral fertilizers that were becoming a big source of wealth as farming industrialized in Europe and North America.

Equipped with modern European weapons, Chile won handily. Bolivia, whose cavalry rode mules and fielded soldiers using flintlock muskets, lost her entire coastline. (Poor Bolivia—over the years, every one of her neighbors has grabbed a chunk of her.) Most of the pisco-producing regions of Peru were occupied, from Tacna all the way to Lima.

The war still lends a bitter note to Peru's relations with Chile. The occupation of Lima lasted from 1881 to 1883. The city was a lawless cauldron of mob rule and was looted mercilessly by Chilean troops, who took much of Peru's cultural patrimony, including nearly all the books in the national library. Tacna was not returned to Peru until 1929, when the southernmost part of Peru, around Arica, was permanently ceded to Chile.

To compound these political disasters, markets in Peru were changing. Poorer Peruvians were developing a taste for rum—*aguardiente de caña* or *cañazo*—a much cheaper product from cane-growing areas in the north that became increasingly available as coastal railway lines were completed and colonial-era restrictions on its production were forgotten.

At the same time, the Bolivian mining industry was in a state of collapse, destroying the pisco market there. The southern pisco-growing regions—Arequipa, Moquegua, and Locumba—lost their main market, and many vineyards were converted to growing food crops. It was the last in a series of blows for Moquegua, which had been leveled in 1868 by a powerful earthquake and invaded by Chilean forces four times during the war.

Things only got worse in the 1880s, when phylloxera, the insect pest that had been ravaging vineyards worldwide, arrived in Peru. Its effect was to further concentrate production in Ica where, thanks to the topography and abundant water supply, the practice had long been to irrigate the vines by flooding the vineyards a few times each season—a method that just happens to drown the parasites in the vines' roots.

NEW BLOOD

In spite of this relentless series of calamities, the return of sovereignty in 1883 heralded the beginning of a bright period for pisco, at least in the region from Lima to Ica. Besides the resumption of normal trading, an even more important element was the arrival of a wave of new immigrants to Peru from Italy.

In the 1880s, the various states of the Italian Peninsula were united as a single nation for the first time since the Roman era. However, Italian unification was a process of upheaval, and it initiated a century of waves of emigration. The first surge, from unification in 1881 to about 1900, comprised some seven million people. Tens of thousands, mostly from the north, came to Peru, partly in response to official Peruvian overtures to Italians.

This influx transformed Peru. Among modern-day Peruvians, Italy is the second most-common European mother country (after Spain). Many Italian immigrants became shopkeepers or traders; some became bankers; yet others brought their fishing skills to the rich Peruvian waters. Some, like alembique-maker Don Amoretti's ancestors, brought highly specialized skills. Experienced winemakers sailed directly to Pisco, indelibly transforming Peruvian pisco-making.

The Italians brought sophisticated viticultural knowledge, new grapes, new techniques, and rigorous standards

to the sleepy, centuries-old wine and pisco industries in Peru. Many of today's biggest pisco companies were founded by Italians during this period.

These include Santiago Queirolo, the largest producer in Peru, which was founded in 1885 in Magdalena, an agricultural area near Lima. Today, the bodega is located in the pleasant neighborhood of Pueblo Libre, part of Lima's urban sprawl, and its grapes are grown elsewhere.

When the Italian immigrants arrived on the scene, they added their own novel ways of pisco-drinking to the already well-established local practices. Perhaps the most enduring of these additions is the Chilcano, a tall, refreshing drink made by mixing pisco with ginger ale, bitters and a little lime juice.

The drink purportedly takes its name from a fish-head soup that was said to be a hangover remedy, eaten in the morning after a long night of revelry. Another old Peruvian hangover cure was the last shot of pisco or the early morning shot. The Chilcano—the drink—is the best of both worlds: nourishing and refreshing like the soup, but with the addition of pisco. (Another theory about its origin says the chilcano is named after the town of Chilco, south of Lima.)

SAN FRANCISCO'S TASTE FOR PISCO

The reinvigoration of Peruvian pisco with this infusion of new, Italian blood coincided with a boom in one of pisco's

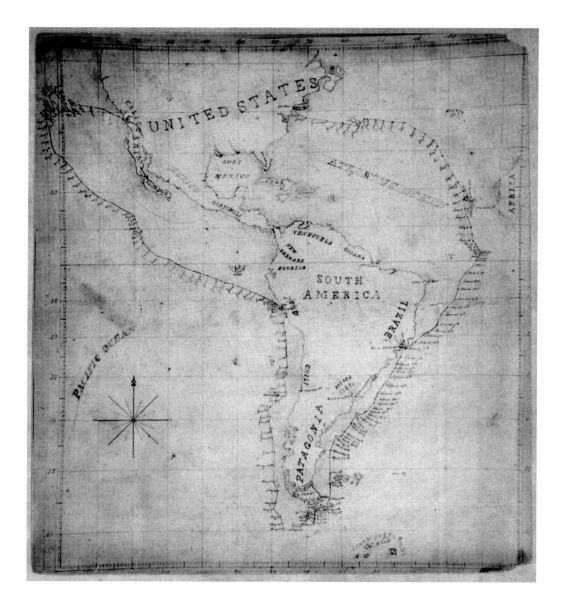

Peru was a stop on the sea journey from the American Eastern Seaboard to California, and many forty-niners passed through. Naturally, they picked up pisco.

most important export markets: the United States, specifically San Francisco. From 1848 to 1849, the city had been the gateway to the California Gold Rush, boosting its population from about 1,000 to 25,000 in a matter of months. In its first few decades San Francisco was a lawless, disorganized boomtown, the whiff of fortunes to be made in the foggy, muddy streets and the threat of vigilante violence and other thuggery around every corner. Cholera epidemics and earthquakes kept things interesting. It's no surprise that drink (not to mention opium) was popular there.

The Gold Rush attracted people from all over the world, including many from Peru, for centuries a worldwide leader in mining precious metals and a relatively easy sea journey away. Callao, Lima's port, was also a stop on the arduous sea journey from the American Eastern Seaboard to California, and many forty-niners passed through on the way.

Naturally, they picked up pisco, which was a common item on vessels sailing the Pacific (Herman Melville wrote about it lovingly in short stories based on his time aboard a New England whaler in the 1840s). San Francisco had a taste for it right from the start: even before 1849 "pisco" and "Italia" in "jars"—that is, botijas—were common items listed in ships' cargos arriving in the port.

Many San Franciscans themselves originally came from Peru, including Domingo Ghirardelli, an Italian chocolate-maker who had been making chocolate in Lima for years before opening his famous factory in San Francisco in 1852. His friend James Lick, a Lima piano manufacturer from Pennsylvania, also moved to San Francisco and, thanks to his real estate acumen, eventually became the wealthiest man in California.

By the 1890s, San Francisco had become the cultural capital of the American West, intent on turning itself into the "Paris of the West." (Never mind the outbreak of bubonic plague in 1900.) The city was on the worldwide itineraries of superstars like Italian tenor Enrique Caruso and the great writers of the age. It featured pleasure parks, theaters, grand hotels, and, of course, opulent bars.

It was the age of American "mixology," in which celebrity bartenders like "Professor" Jerry Thomas (the father of American mixology, who did a couple of stints behind bars in San Francisco) and William "Cocktail" Boothby (who presided over the bar at San Francisco's Palace Hotel) attracted devoted followings for their complex cocktails of exotic ingredients.

The most famous bar in San Francisco at the time was the Bank Exchange, an establishment on Montgomery Street on the site of what is now the city's iconic Transamerica Pyramid.

Founded in 1853 in the brand-new Montgomery Block, a building that housed offices and shops, the Bank Exchange exuded elegance and sophistication in a city where such things were in distinctly short supply. By 1858 San Francisco's newspapers were running ads for the Bank Exchange, which, in addition to listing billiard supplies and "all the choicest brands of champagne," announced that the establishment carried "on hand and for sale… Apple Jack, Pisco, Arrac, Cordials, Liquors, Etc, Etc, Etc."

The Bank Exchange catered to the bankers and stock traders who lived and worked in the neighborhood. The stock exchange was nearby, and the Bank of Italy, later known as the Bank of America, was in the same building. Wells Fargo was around the corner.

Despite various changes of ownership and a bankruptcy, the Bank Exchange became a fixture in the city, but it was by no means the only bar in San Francisco to serve pisco. The Mansion House, next to Mission Dolores, for example, was known for milk punches made with pisco, a typical mixture in Peru at the time. Plus, weekend bullfights and bear-baiting spectacles were held out front, recreating a recipe for entertainment—bullfighting and pisco milk punches—that had been popular in Lima for a century or more. It was, accordingly, a favorite hangout of the city's Latin American population.

The Bank Exchange, however, was the place rich and famous Anglos went to drink pisco. It was celebrated by many visitors to San Francisco, including Mark Twain and Rudyard Kipling. Both authors were known for an enthusiasm for fine drink that set them apart, even in a profession renowned for its enduring affinity with the sauce. In 1864 Twain, who frequented the Bank Exchange regularly, wrote about the place. (He also spent time at a nearby Turkish bath, where he was attended by a fireman named Tom Sawyer.)

But the most eloquent of the surviving accounts of the bar comes from Rudyard Kipling in 1889. Among his many other distinctions, Kipling was the popularizer of the Pegu Club Cocktail, as prepared at his beloved Pegu Club in Rangoon. He wrote about San Francisco in his travelogue *From Sea to Sea*. Wedged between an account of a murder he witnessed in Chinatown and a discussion of the widespread practice of wholesale vote-buying, Kipling describes stopping for a draught at the Bank Exchange:

> In the heart of the business quarter, where banks and bankers are thickest, and telegraph wires most numerous, stands a semi-subterranean bar tended by a German with long blond locks and a crystalline eye. Go thither softly, treading on the tips of your toes, and ask him for a Button Punch. 'Twill take ten minutes to brew, but the result is the highest and noblest product of the age. No man but one knows what is in it. I have a theory that it is compounded of the shavings of cherubs' wings, the glory of a tropical dawn, the red clouds of sunset, and fragments of lost epics by dead masters. But try you for yourselves, and pause a while to bless me, who am always mindful of the truest interests of my brethren.

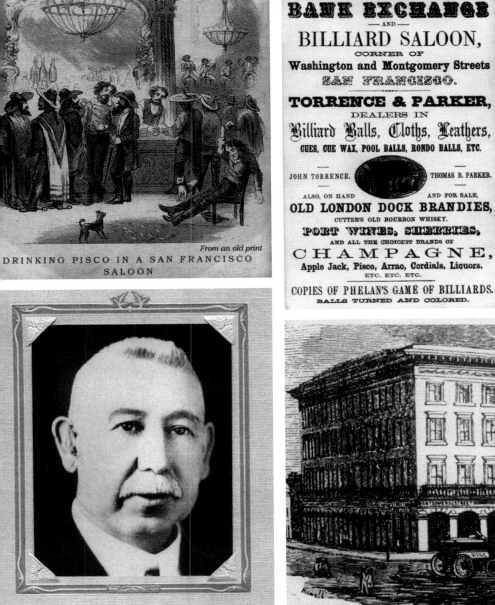

DRINKING PISCO IN A SAN FRANCISCO
SALOON

From an old print

BANK EXCHANGE
— AND —
BILLIARD SALOON,
CORNER OF
Washington and Montgomery Streets
SAN FRANCISCO.

TORRENCE & PARKER,
DEALERS IN
Billiard Balls, Cloths, Leathers,
CUES, CUE WAX, POOL BALLS, RONDO BALLS, ETC.

JOHN TORRENCE.   THOMAS B. PARKER.

ALSO, ON HAND   AND FOR SALE,

OLD LONDON DOCK BRANDIES,
CUTTER'S OLD BOURBON WHISKY.

PORT WINES, SHERRIES,
AND ALL THE CHOICEST BRANDS OF
CHAMPAGNE,
Apple Jack, Pisco, Arrac, Cordials, Liquors,
ETC. ETC. ETC.

COPIES OF PHELAN'S GAME OF BILLIARDS.
BALLS TURNED AND COLORED.

Thanks to this kind of press, the Bank Exchange became a requisite stop on any cultured traveler's visit to San Francisco. It's not known what Kipling's Button Punch contained, but many suppose it was pisco. At the time Kipling visited, one Duncan Nicol, a young Scotsman who had started working there as a teenager, was behind the bar. In 1893, at the age of thirty, he became the co-proprietor of the Bank Exchange and soon became famous for his Pisco Punch.

THE MYSTERY OF NICOL'S PISCO PUNCH

Punch is one of the oldest types of mixed drinks, traditionally including liquor, sugar, fruit, water, and flavorings. The name comes from the Hindi for "five"—as in five ingredients—as the formulation was brought to Europe from India by the intrepid English, who first wrote about it in 1632. Prior to Nicol's concoction, pisco punches had been enjoyed elsewhere for years—the earliest written account dates to 1791 when a Lima newspaper described the drinks sold at the bullring there.

Nonetheless, Nicol's drink stands out. The recipe was top secret—Nicol allowed only his deaf-mute assistant in the back room while he prepared it—but its properties were legendary. "One authority claims one punch 'will make a gnat fight an elephant.' Others maintain it floats them in the region of bliss of hasheesh and absinthe," wrote Pauline Jacobson in a 1912 pamphlet about the Bank Exchange. By then, Nicol was so renowned for this one drink that he was known as "Pisco John." ("John" came from the telephone number of the bar in 1903).

And the bar's fame reached new heights after 1906, the year the great earthquake and fire leveled much of San Francisco. It remains the biggest disaster ever to have befallen an American city, yet it spared the Montgomery Block, and the Bank Exchange became celebrated as one of the few remainders of "old" San Francisco, a "temple of the past" as Pauline Jacobson put it. The place was an institution: the three things that every visitor to San Francisco "had" to do were ride the cable cars, watch the sun set through the Golden Gate, and try Duncan Nicol's Pisco Punch.

But even the Bank Exchange could not withstand the bureaucratic calamity that followed in 1920—Prohibition. The bar was shuttered, and Duncan Nicol died six years later, taking the secret of his Pisco Punch with him to the grave.

THE BIRTH OF THE PISCO SOUR

Prohibition was a multifaceted disaster for drinking in the United States (that was the point), and pisco imports from Peru dried up utterly. But one of the unintended consequences of Prohibition is that it dispersed American-style cocktail knowledge around the world, as professional mixologists took their craft elsewhere. It also enriched the cocktail oeuvre, by exposing these seasoned barmen to new in-

OPPOSITE: The House of Pisco, which was on the 500 block of Pacific Street in San Francisco, during its heyday in 1942.

gredients in other lands, a burst of creativity that gave the world the Bloody Mary and many other classics, thanks to a cadre of expat bartenders (and thirsty writers) at Harry's New York Bar in Paris.

A similar thing happened in Peru. Victor Morris was born in 1873 in Salt Lake City, Utah. He came from a family of prominent Mormons (his father had come West with Brigham Young) yet they also had a wild side: In 1899, Morris' brother was murdered over the fatal combination of a woman and a badly made Mint Julep. (Six of them, actually.)

In 1903, Morris, who had been working in the auditing department of the Oregon Short Line Railroad, was taken on as a cashier for the Cerro de Pasco Railway Company in Peru. The company, run by Utah railroad men, some of whom knew Morris, was building railroads in the Andes during one of the frequent mining booms there.

Tombstone of Victor Morris, creator of the Pisco Sour, in the English Cemetery just outside Lima.

Morris shipped out to Peru from San Francisco. A Mormon who nonetheless liked his drink, he likely stopped at the Bank Exchange on his way through the city, although there is no evidence of this one way or the other.

Thirteen years later, having completed his work in the mountains, Morris repaired to Lima, where there were sizeable British and American populations. There, he opened Morris' Bar on a tony street called Jirón de la Unión. It quickly became favored by the booming Anglo enclave in Lima—nine out of ten people who signed the bar's register were English-speaking foreigners.

Morris, who had been known for his amateur bartending skills in Salt Lake City, had naturally begun experimenting with pisco shortly after his arrival in Peru. But it was at the Morris' Bar that he made his name as the inventor of the drink that was to become the national drink of Peru—the Pisco Sour.

(It's true: the country has a national cocktail. By law it is served at any diplomatic function held in Peru or her embassies and consulates around the world.)

The exact origin of the Pisco Sour is not totally certain. One theory holds that early in his Peruvian career Morris substituted lime and pisco for the lemon and whiskey in the Whiskey Sour. Another, more nuanced theory persuasively advanced by Guillermo Toro-Lira, a Peruvian-American historian whose work is the basis for much of this chapter, is that Morris based the recipe not on the American sour, but on the fizz. At any rate, it was clear that he was in touch with American mixologists (in 1925 John Lannes, who had worked as a bartender at the Bank Exchange, signed the register at Morris' Bar) and was following their methods for high-end cocktails.

For example, Morris used gum arabic in some of his drinks. The sap of an African acacia, gum arabic lends mouthfeel to a cocktail, and has the added benefit of blocking the taste of alcohol from the tongue, letting a drink combine delicate flavors with a real punch, as it were.

By 1924 the popularity of the pisco sour had spread beyond Peru. An advertisement for Morris' Bar published in an English-language weekly in Valparaíso, Chile in that year lists the Pisco Sour along with many cocktails that had been popular in the United States prior to Prohibition (although not, it should be noted, the Mint Julep).

THE GOOD TIMES

Morris died in 1929 (cirrhosis, naturally), but his recipe survived in the hands of Mario Bruiget, his young assistant. Already a highly regarded barman, Bruiget was snapped up by the nearby Hotel Maury, where he may have substituted the cheaper, and similarly unctuous, egg white for gum arabic and created the classic Pisco Sour. (Nobody knows for certain how Morris made his Pisco Sours—there is some evidence that his recipe changed over time—but it is clear that by the time the Maury became known for them the canonical recipe had emerged.)

Bruiget also helped launch the Maury into the top ranks of Peruvian drinking establishments, helping the Pisco Sour become *the* way to drink pisco in Peru. The drink is a robust combination of distinctively Peruvian flavors: pisco Quebranta, the distinctive bitter Peruvian lime, and a bouquet of bitters from the drops floated on top of the egg white foam. The Pisco Sour is Peru in a glass.

(Many bitters, including Angostura, are based on cinchona, the bark of a tree native to the Peruvian Amazon—it was also known as "Peruvian bark." In the nineteenth century it was a wonder drug, heralded worldwide for its ability to cure malaria—a scourge of humankind for millennia. Quinine, its active ingredient, is the base bitterness in tonic water, some vermouths, and the aforementioned bitters—all of which were originally formulated as medicines. The cinchona tree appears on the Peruvian coat of arms—take a look.)

Today, the big, beautiful mahogany bar at the Maury seems tired: bartenders who don't know better laconically crank out overly acidic, warm Pisco Sours for tourists who have no way of knowing how bad the pisco is they are drinking. But in its heyday, the Maury was a central part of Lima's—and modern Peru's—golden age.

During World War I, a big mineral boom began when Europeans needed seemingly endless supplies of guano and nitrates for making bombs. A parallel cotton boom spread through the fertile valleys of Peru's coast. American money in particular flowed into Lima as that nation asserted its Monroe Doctrine and replaced the European powers as the dominant imperial force in South America.

Peru's international stature was growing; the 1913 announcement of Hiram Bingham's "discovery" of Machu Picchu set off a wave of international interest in this exotic land. Meanwhile, relative political stability allowed the economy to further blossom.

Yet it was a period of contraction for pisco. Cotton replaced pisco grapes as a crop in many areas, and the acreage shrank and concentrated even more around Ica, accelerating the substitution of cane liquor for pisco among the masses. Still, this was Peru's golden age, and it mattered little to the moneyed classes and growing bourgeoisie in Lima what the poor were drinking—there was still plenty of pisco poured at the fine hotels and clubs springing up throughout the city.

In 1924, flush with cash and pride—rarely an enduring combination—the government of Peru set about an ambitious plan to modernize Lima for the occasion of the nation's centennial. The downtown was remodeled in grand beaux-arts style on the model of Haussmann's Paris. One of the jewels of the project was the Gran Hotel Bolívar, an enormous white wedding cake on the Plaza San Martín.

The hotel instantly became the center of upper-class *Limeño* social life. There, international stars like Ernest Hemingway (there for the fishing) became acquainted with creamy, strong Pisco Sours served in giant "cathedral" glasses. (Indeed, the opening of the Bolívar ushered in the decline of Morris' Bar, as the glitzy hotel attracted the same core clientele, and even some of its bartenders.)

Another classic cocktail, the Capitán, gained currency among Lima's elite at the Bolívar. A blend of pisco and sweet vermouth, it was so-named because it combined the red and white of a Peruvian captain's stripe. The Capitán Cocktail may have originated in response to the contraction in supply of American whiskey during Prohibition, making Manhattans much more difficult to make. A competing theory holds that it was yet another Italian innovation.

Served straight up in a small glass, at ambient temperature, the Capitán was a winter drink—smooth and warming in Lima's relentlessly gray months. (The drink later fell out of favor, becoming known as an old man's drink, although of late it has been revived somewhat thanks to frequent mention in one of Mario Vargas Llosa's novels.)

TROUBLE ABROAD

During these good times, the Peruvian mood was perhaps a little overconfident. Peruvians barely noticed when in 1931 Chile established Denomination of Origin for "pisco" made in northern Chile. The move by the commercially canny Chileans was designed to boost demand for Chilean aguardiente de uva in Europe by associating it with the famous name "pisco." In 1936, the Chileans went so far as to change the name of the town of La Unión to Pisco Elqui in order to bolster their claim.

Really, Chilean "pisco" is an altogether different liquor from Peruvian pisco: it is made from different grapes; it may contain cane sugar; it is distilled to high proof in a column still then rectified with water; and it is aged in oak barrels, which give it a light coloring. It has a different flavor and different standards, yet to foreigners in distant lands the distinction is obscure.

In the 1930s nearly the entire production of pisco in Peru was consumed domestically, and producers and consumers cared little for the antics of the perfidious Chileans. Yet Peruvian lassitude was to come back to haunt them, as Chilean pisco came to define the liquor in many important markets, to the extent that even many Chileans don't know that pisco is not from Chile, making its origins a contentious flashpoint that can stand in for the whole suite of rivalries between the two countries.

Anyway, Peruvians soon had other preoccupations. The worldwide depression of 1929 blew apart the golden age and brought back chronic political instability. The 1930s saw a wave of violent repression of bourgeoning leftist political movements, with tens of thousands killed or imprisoned.

THE BAD TIMES

After World War II, in spite of a post-war boom in South America, Peru endured a series of bruising political struggles between military oligarchs and leftist and populist movements. Massive demographic shifts were taking place as well, as the agrarian nation's industrial base grew, attracting poor, largely indigenous migrants to Lima.

Still, the party continued unabated at the Bolívar into the 1960s, but the hotel now had competition. In 1925, the year after the Bolívar opened, ground was broken for the Hotel Country Club in San Isidro, an upscale district on the edge of Lima. This marked a subtle change in the center of gravity for Lima's elite that eventually became a rush, as the wealthy and the powerful abandoned the city center during the decades after World War II in favor of the sprawling suburbanization of San Isidro and Miraflores, by the seaside. Unintentionally, Lima, which had styled itself after Paris, came to resemble Los Angeles.

Today, the Country Club's Bar Inglés is an elegant watering hole for Lima's elite, while the Bolívar, like the nearby Maury, is a somewhat shabby spot where tourists and poor-

Chilean "pisco" is an altogether different liquor from Peruvian pisco: it is made from different grapes; it may contain cane sugar; it is distilled to high proof then diluted with water; and it is aged in oak barrels, which gives it a light coloring. It has a different flavor and different standards.

er, decidedly darker-complexioned Limeños gather under fluorescent lights for inferior Pisco Sours.

In the 1970s, the socialist dictatorship of Juan Velasco Alvarado instituted a program of radical land reform, taking huge holdings away from the families who in many cases had owned them since the conquest, and redistributing them to landless peasants. While greater equity in the distribution of land and wealth was about a millennium overdue in Peru, the way it was done collapsed the agricultural sector.

Pisco was not spared. The great haciendas of the Ica valley and elsewhere were broken up. "It was a black moment for Peru," Rodolfo Mejía told me, shaking his head, as I sipped pisco with him at the remains of his family's ancient estate.

Doña Juanita agreed, "Since the agrarian reform it has all gone downhill. Everything has been mistreated. The workers became the owners, but they didn't really know how to use these things or take care of them; a lot of them just tried to sell them." (Unlike don Mejía, though, her alacrity for making lemons into lemonade served her well: "We took advantage of that opportunity and bought our old paila with the gold in it—they didn't know what they had!")

The situation got even worse in the 1980s when Peru's boom sector was cocaine. The industry brought with it extreme violence on all sides and fanned simmering ethnic and class tensions into what amounted to a civil war between the

central government and the Maoist Shining Path movement.

After two centuries of indignities, this was perhaps the worst period of all for pisco. Quality plummeted, and even among the elite pisco became known as the choice beverage of drunks.

Ironically, this deterioration in quality also cemented the Pisco Sour as the national drink: of all the classic pisco cocktails, the Pisco Sour is the most forgiving in the face of inferior pisco. By changing the ratio of ingredients to boost the lime and sugar, desperate barmen were able to continue serving the drink. Indeed, it was even said that the best Pisco Sours were made using the worst pisco—an assertion that can only be the product of resignation and complete ignorance of the balance and subtlety of good pisco.

ABOVE: Lima's Country Club, home of the famous Bar Inglés.

OPPOSITE: The bar at Lima's Hotel Maury, one of the spots that helped make the Pisco Sour into Peru's national cocktail. Note the painting of tipplers dancing the marinera, a domesticated descendant of the zamacueca.

5

Jaranas, el Corte, and Macerados
Pisco Style and Pisco Culture

It's almost impossible to go to Peru and not drink pisco. Every time I visit, I find myself in front of a Pisco Sour within 12 hours, tops. Even George W. Bush, a well-known teetotaler, was photographed quaffing one of the national cocktails during a summit meeting in Lima.

It's always been that way. Alcoholic beverages are a deep-rooted tradition in the Americas. In Peru, long before the arrival of the Spaniards, the natives drank *chicha*, a fermented beverage made from corn or other starches and flavored with fruits and herbs. For many cultures, including the Incas, chicha had important ritual and religious significance. Outside homes in the Inca heartland around Cuzco you can still see long poles holding aloft small flags, indicating that chicha is for sale.

When the Spanish conquerors arrived, the substitution of the grape—central to the Catholic religion—was not a huge leap. Indeed, many of the Peruvian tools and practices surrounding wine and pisco—including botijas and the habit of dropping a bit on the ground for Pachamama, the Andean Earth goddess—are variations on older ones involving chicha.

But because of its association with indigenous religion and culture, the Spaniards took a dim view of chicha, and tried to suppress it: in 1594, for example, the Crown declared a (futile) ban on it. At times, the civil and religious authorities banned all alcoholic drinks for native peoples (except sacramental wine, presumably) on the grounds that they had a tendency towards blind drunkenness that made them ineffective indentured laborers and unconvincing Christians.

But if the indigenous population had good reason to drown their sorrows, they by no means had a monopoly on drunkenness in the Viceroyalty. In 1616, Pedro de León Portocarrero, a trader known as the Portuguese Jew, visited Lima and described huge, wild parties fueled by wine, chicha, and *guarapo* (fermented sugar cane juice). Later visitors only confirmed that inebriation was a part of the fabric of Lima life. In 1630, there were at least 250 bars and taverns where alcohol was served—one for every hundred inhabitants—in spite of efforts by the authorities to limit them.

PARTYING LIKE IT'S 1899
In the highlands, pisco joined chicha as a central part of many communal events, leading to long, alcohol-steeped revelries that lasted for days. In his 1846 account of life in Peru, the Swiss doctor Johann Jakob von Tschudi wrote of drunkenness at all levels of society, ranging from villagers;

> "Every one of their often-recurring festivals is celebrated by a drinking bout, at which enormous quantities of

brandy [i.e. pisco] and chicha are consumed."

To indigenous miners;

> "When excited by strong drinks, such as… chicha and brandy… the Indian miners… go about the streets rioting and attacking each other."

To the respectable classes;

> "The quantity of brandy drunk at one of the evening parties called in the Sierra *Jaranas*, is almost incredible. According to my observation, I should say that a bottle to each individual, ladies included, is a fair average estimate, the bottles being the size of those in Europe used for claret…[At one party thrown for a Chilean General,] the brandy flowed in such quantities, that, when morning came, some members of the company were found lying on the floor of the ball-room in a state of intoxication."

Notwithstanding the good doctor's somewhat prim attitude to these blowouts, it sounds like the *jaranas* were a lot of fun. The largest were massive gatherings of ten thousand people or more held outside Lima, where revelers ate and drank for days, smoking like chimneys and dancing the *zamacueca* to the boisterous combination of harp, guitar, and *cajón*.

An energetic, graceful, and sensual pas de deux that originated among coastal Afro-Peruvians but soon spread to everyone, the zamacueca was always soaked in pisco—dancers ritualistically downed shots before, during, and after the dance, and many of the songs were even odes to pisco.

The biggest jarana, the Fiesta de Amancaes, took place every year outside Lima at the time of the blossoming of the *amancaes* flower, a wildflower something like a daffodil. It was held putatively to celebrate the feast of Saint John the Baptist, a feast day that many formerly pagan cultures have found conveniently coincides with the summer solstice. It famously included members of all levels of society and served as a melting pot for cultural transference, where food, drink, and song (and no doubt a lot more) were shared across class and race.

While contemporary commentators and many modern observers too claim that the energy for these all-night festivities of sweaty dancing came from the pisco itself, there are other possibilities as well. For centuries in Peru, pisco has been used as the base for *macerados*, infusions in which different fruits and herbs are steeped in pisco, lending the liquor their color, flavor, and properties.

For centuries at bars, at jaranas, and in private homes alike, countless macerados were prepared, some with a single ingredient and others with more complex mixtures. Common items for maceration included dried fruit, nuts, and orange peel. Pineapple rind was another classic, and macerations that included cinchona (Peruvian bark) and coca were frequently employed as bitters.

Straight macerados of coca leaves were widespread. A nutritious, energy-giving plant that has been used for millennia in the Andes, coca is more widely known as the source of cocaine. When steeped in alcohol, the leaves render a potent energy drink that has the effect of completely banishing the sense of fatigue that is otherwise the inevitable result of hours — or days — of partying.

Getting down at a Jarana—a wild pisco-fueled party.

PISCO IN DAILY LIFE

Throughout all of Peru's ups and downs, from the early colonial period to today, the Limeño café scene never let up. More bars than cafés, Lima's taverns were known for *bu-*

tifarras—sandwiches of succulent, thick ham—and pisco puro. As happens in any great city, some were known as places where bigwigs discussed politics, some as gathering spots for artistic bohemians, some as dens of lowlifes.

A few in this style still remain—Santiago Queirolo maintains a rather spotlessly clean one (old accounts report they were anything but), the Antigua Taberna Queirolo, on the corner of the block where they run their bodega in Lima. It is an inviting, high-ceilinged space with tall, ornate shelves of polished, dark wood holding bottles of all manner of grape products—pisco, of course, but also wine, sparkling wine, and brandy. In glass cases, big trays are heaped with savory delicacies like pickled vegetables, ceviche, pigs' feet, and potato salad. Hams, cheeses, and bottles of beer share space behind the long marble counter.

Pisco accompanied the good times for every social class: it was drunk at bullfights (often as punch), cockfights (*puro*, or straight up), and gatherings of rich owners of Paso horses. (The handsome Peruvian Paso horse has a distinctive trotting gait. One traditional measure of a rider's skill is the ability to hold a glass of pisco in one hand while riding, and never spill a drop.)

Throughout Peru, especially on the coast, a custom known as *las once*—the elevens—was faithfully observed. This consisted of a pre-lunch tipple of pisco puro (straight pisco) accompanied by olives or other snacks. Some say it gained its name because of the time of day at which it was enjoyed, others because the word "aguardiente" has eleven letters in it.

This association of pisco with all the good things in life—camaraderie, food, art, dancing, music, sport, and entertainment—marked pisco as an ineradicable part of the Peruvian identity. And it was nowhere more so than in the pisco-producing regions themselves.

While many visitors enjoyed the party scene in Lima, few went to Ica, tending to agree with Reginaldo de Lizárraga, who in 1609 described it as a good place to "fill up your flask and keep going."

Yet if visitors had stayed longer, they would have discovered a whole other world of traditional pisco-drinking—that associated with the production of pisco itself. Every important (and even unimportant) part of the pisco-making process involves a few shots of the stuff: from pruning the vines to stomping the grapes to distilling the mosto, no step starts without a stiff draught of pisco puro.

Usually, it was drunk in a *caña*, a stout tumbler that held four fingers of pisco, like the one don Mejía shared with us. It's named after the length of cane traditionally used to sample pisco from botijas.

Don Mejía explained some more of the customs to me while we sat in the dappled shade of the bamboo awning in front of his house. "Generally we drank it in the morn-

For centuries pisco was the base for macerados, infusions in which different fruits and herbs are steeped in pisco, lending the liquor their color, flavor, and properties. Macerados of coca leaves were widespread. Mayta, a restaurant in Lima, is leading a macerado rediscovery with its inventive and delicious concoctions, at left.

ing, with lime," he said, speaking of his young adulthood. "Not at las once—earlier! To open the appetite. In the winter it is raw here, so we drank it with lime to avoid the cold."

The morning drink is called *el corte*—the cut—and is to be taken first thing, with nothing more than a little lime, if desired. It, of course, has supposed health benefits, with aficionados claiming that it reduces cholesterol, boosts energy, opens the blood vessels, improves brain function, increases appetite, aids digestion, and—somehow at the same time—is slimming.

This health talk goes hand in hand with a Peruvian obsession with avoiding hangovers through, ironically, drinking pisco. Besides the Chilcano, traditionally drunk as a morning-after remedy, there was a corte downed at the end of a night of partying or upon waking. And, as any pisco connoisseur will tell you, a hangover is the result of inferior pisco—many claim it is impossible to get a hangover from pure, high-quality pisco.

Workers could not see the point of going out into the fields unfortified by pisco. And, of course, upon returning, there was the afternoon dram too. There were also plenty of ways to mix pisco. *Vino Dulce* was a blend of pisco and grape juice. A *Chinguero* was pisco with fresh orange and grape

juice. "It is very agreeable," said don Mejía. "We also drank something called *Orina del Niño* [the urine of the Christ child] at Christmastime—it was made with cinnamon and cloves and the juice of young grapes. You cook that, and then add pisco. We made macerados with wild cherries and apricots."

THE PAST IN A GLASS

Doña Juanita at Tres Generaciones is keeping alive some of these old concoctions. She serves a wide range of interesting macerados at her restaurant, including cocktails made with them, and she knows how to prescribe them too. *Macerado de hierba luisa* (lemongrass) is good for colic. *Macerado de ruda* (rue) keeps away the bad vibes. Her *macerado de coca* is the best we found in Peru; sweetened with a touch of huarango honey, it's smooth and silky, with a pleasing vegetal flavor but none of the bitterness that macerados de coca can sometimes have. And, it is astonishingly effective, keeping one's head clear late into the night regardless of the quantities of pisco consumed.

She also serves an excellent Algarrobina. A traditional pisco cocktail that is the last remaining milk-based cocktail in the classic pisco repertoire, the Algarrobina is like a heavy pisco milkshake, featuring an egg yolk and syrup from huarango or carob seeds. It's supposed to be a lady's cocktail, but, properly made, it's a meal in itself.

Unlike many of the people that color the history of

OPPOSITE:
top: Doña Juanita's macerados; *middle:* Straining coca macerated pisco; *bottom:* Mayta bartender offers a chilcano and coca infused pisco puro.

pisco, doña Juanita is not protective of her recipes. "It's not a secret," she told us. "I don't keep secrets from people who want to learn."

Tres Generaciones also continues to make an even rarer traditional form of flavored pisco, *pisco aromatizado*, in which fruits other than grapes have been added to the mosto. She prepares her *pisco cereza* by suspending a basket of fresh cherries inside the falca as the mosto cooks (thanks to Peruvian topography it is possible to get fresh ripe cherries from the Ica highlands shortly after the grape harvest in the lowlands). We tried one that had been aged for five years; it was kissed with a hint of color, and had a rich flavor of dried fruit, almost like a fruitcake. Best of all, it left us with an aftertaste as though we had just eaten a bowl of perfect, juicy, ripe cherries.

Another version flavored with limes was, to our taste, less successful—it came out a bit antiseptic, though resolutely traditional. "Pisco and lime have always gone together," said doña Juanita. "They both came with the Spanish—they are brothers."

In March during the grape harvest, Ica hosts a big festival devoted to all things from the vine called La Vendímia. It's a huge party reminiscent of the old jaranas, with all-night revelry and lots of drinking. It is also the occasion for smaller parties at the bodegas, as bare-legged men and women leap into big patios piled high with grapes and sys-

tematically stomp them to release the juice. They are, naturally, rewarded with frequent pisco shots. They also enjoy draughts of *Chinguerito*, fresh grape juice mixed with pisco, and sometimes flavored with lime, cinnamon, and cloves.

The blaring amplified music, bright lights, and chattering cell phones at La Vendímia, however, make one long for the old jaranas, with their lively zamacuecas and spirited horsemanship. These massive parties faded in the twentieth century alas, with the last, tame versions sputtering out in the 1950s. The fields of amancaes outside of Lima, once carpeted with flowers, were lost to the city's sprawl, just as the multiple and diverse ways of drinking pisco were drowned in an ocean of mediocre Pisco Sours. Today, more than 70 percent of all pisco produced in Peru is consumed in Pisco Sours. Every February, on the first Saturday, Peru celebrates Pisco Sour Day, but it is no substitute for what has been lost.

Yet even in that hegemonic cocktail, we can taste the past: the lime that has gone hand in hand with pisco since the beginning. Even the sugar and the egg white were traditional adjuncts to certain pisco drinks. And the bitters are a remorseful whiff of the world of macerados that lubricated the not-so-distant past.

And then there's the pisco itself: an eau de vie of grapes, the original distilled spirit. To this day it is still made in antique copper stills, approaching the earliest distilled alcohols of nearly a millennium ago more closely than any other liquor on the market today.

OPPOSITE:
left: Local pisco-maker sharing his pisco at La Vendímia; *top middle:* Revelers enjoying the Marisól concert at La Vendímia; *middle middle:* Accepting the crown as the La Vendímia Queen; *bottom-middle:* Revelers at La Vendímia; *top right:* Future La Vendímia princesses performing traditional dances; *bottom right:* One of the bodegas' tasting areas at La Vendímia.

6

Putting It Back Together Again
The New Generation and the Pisco Renaissance

The first time I had the opportunity to travel to Peru, I stood by the shore of Lake Titicaca in Bolivia, too scared to put my foot across the border and make a two-day dash for Machu Picchu. It was 1989, and the Shining Path, Peru's violent Maoist insurgency, had developed a habit of nabbing foreigners off rural buses and making them vanish. Fast-forward twenty years, and Peru is one of the most delightful places in the world for visitors—it's been an incredible transformation.

Peru started the new millennium in a precarious state of affairs. The "internal conflict"— a civil war between the government and insurgents—was winding down. The economy was a shambles; corruption was rampant even by Peruvian standards; tourism was nonexistent; and the political situation was a mess. Something like 70,000 people—mostly poor highland civilians of indigenous extraction—had been killed since 1980 in the bloodiest conflict in Peru since the Spanish conquest. There was much healing to do, on every front.

But if there is any lesson from Peruvian history, it is that the pendulum swings both ways. In the years following 2000, Peru got back on her feet remarkably quickly. New natural gas developments pumped huge amounts of cash into the economy, while a relatively convincing democracy reappeared, even if this did little to alleviate the chronic poverty in much of the Andes. This stability, combined with Peru's longtime position as a major source of minerals, and an end to many of Juan Velasco's socialist economic policies, led to a surge in foreign investment in the country and the highest growth rates in all of Latin America. Even the worldwide slump in 2009 did little more than temper the good times.

THE GASTRONOMIC RENAISSANCE

It was also an era of Peruvian cultural reawakening. Lima, with a growing middle class and a renewed sense of safety, experienced a culinary explosion. Most prominently, Gastón Acurio, a Peruvian chef who had trained at Le Cordon Bleu in Paris, turned his skills towards the diverse culinary heritage of his native land and elevated it to the level of fine dining as "novo-Andino" cuisine.

Peru's varied local ingredients, from climate zones as disparate as coastal desert, high mountain, and tropical rainforest, and multiple cultural antecedents—most notably Inca, Spanish, Italian, Chinese, Japanese, and African— have fostered a unique, wide-ranging, and richly layered cuisine that prizes freshness and deep fusion. Ceviche, the classic dish of raw fish marinated in lime juice and *ají* (chili pepper), is a case in point: it contains echoes of pre-Colum-

Peruvian ceviche made with shrimp and corvina, or sea bass.

bian dishes, but with the addition of limes, a Spanish introduction. In its modern form, it arose at the hands of Japanese chefs employed in the kitchens of Limeño gentry.

Working with this kind of history and the incredible bounty of Peruvian agriculture, Acurio and others spearheaded a rethinking of traditional Peruvian food that, over the past decade, has transformed dining out first in Peru and later in capitals throughout Latin America.

In this context, in which all things traditionally Peruvian received a second look and an infusion of modern technology and sensibilities, pisco began to reawaken. There was a lot of work to be done: at least two generations of Peruvians had learned to shun the stuff, considering it rotgut suitable only for desperate old men. And who could blame them? The overall quality of pisco at the start of the millennium was very poor. Biondi, an old Italian company in Tacna, was the only decent mainstream brand on the market. The rest were frequently adulterated with cane alcohol, or loaded with off flavors from careless fermentation and distillation. Pisco was barely palatable, and only when buried under sugar, lime, and egg in a Pisco Sour.

But a few people knew they could do better. The first major development came as early as 1990, when, in an effort to boost the export of pisco (negligible at the time), Peruvian makers finally started to talk about what they could do to improve standards.

By the mid-1990s, a few serious producers were turning out excellent pisco in this new old style. Viejo Tonel, for example, which began making pisco in Ica in 1997, was the first to reintroduce some of the lesser-known grapes to the market.

William Temoche Solis, Viejo Tonel's president and one of the partners in the business, had been a wine importer. "I sold a lot of imported products, but I had nothing Peruvian," he remembers, "So I got into pisco. I wanted to do something Peruvian, and I had the distribution connections."

Viejo Tonel's bodega is no-nonsense: an open-sided building of brick walls, hemmed in close by vineyards that extend, implausibly, right up onto the sand dunes. It turns out that good pisco needn't come from a centuries-old bodega. "When we introduced these piscos in Peru," he recalls, "consumers saw that they were a rare thing. We took a lot of care with the quality and that is what really set us apart."

The business has been growing ever since: "Since we started," says Temoche, "we have been increasing production each year. And it's still growing: we are buying land, building a new bodega—all that stuff."

THE DENOMINATION OF ORIGIN

At last, in 1999, Peruvians got around to developing their own Denomination of Origin for Peruvian pisco. A denomination is simply a set of rules backed by government authority that defines what is allowed and required for a regional food product to carry a certain name. The concept is ancient—many centuries-old European Royal decrees grant various food monopolies. The modern framework dates to 1925 when the French parliament laid out the rules for what could be called Roquefort cheese. It has since been expanded globally to cover all sorts of foods, most notably wines.

The system works to protect artisanal products from outside imitators by establishing a legal basis for the use of specific names. Usually, the names are related to place, and are exclusive. This creates some awkwardness in the case of pisco, since the Chilean appellation dates to 1931 in spite of the fact that pisco has a far longer documented history in Peru.

Nonetheless, the Chilean appellation was a fait accompli in the major foreign markets of the United States and Europe. Not only was it older, but the Chilean production is around ten times the Peruvian, and it is a monopolistic sector, controlled by two tightly integrated companies. Thus Chilean producers can act quickly and decisively. The Peruvians, who are notorious among themselves for competing rather than cooperating, had little choice but to join the party with their own denomination for Peruvian pisco if they had any hope of becoming known internationally.

The standards developed are remarkably well thought out, as they preserve pisco's traditional strengths while also leaving room for improvement and innovation with modern techniques and technology—and they are exact.

In 1999, Peru developed its own Denomination of Origin for Peruvian pisco — a set of rules that defines what is allowed to be called "pisco".

According to the denomination's definition of Peruvian pisco, it must be produced in one of 42 coastal valleys and distilled entirely from the juice of eight allowable grapes (the four non-aromatics—Quebranta, Mollar, Negra Corriente, and Uvina—and the four aromatics—Moscatel, Torontel, Albilla, and Italia) using the wild yeast found naturally on their skins. It must be created through a single distillation to proof in either a falca or an alembique, with no additives whatsoever—not even water. The liquor must be allowed to rest thereafter for at least three months in nonreactive vessels (traditionally tar or wax-lined ceramics, but now stainless steel or plastic) and must be between 38 percent and 48 percent alcohol. Nothing else can be called pisco.

THE NEW BREED

The growth in new-wave pisco includes producers from many different backgrounds. Some are new entrants like Viejo Tonel and Qollqe, an impeccable boutique brand begun by Cecilia Ledesma, which buys grapes from growers and uses borrowed equipment to yield a tiny production

OPPOSITE: William Temoche Solis, founder and president of Viejo Tonel.

volume. On the other end of the spectrum is Viñas de Oro, a huge company that has taken advantage of its scale to become a major player almost overnight.

Others are small, established producers like Tres Generaciones that had always attended carefully to quality, and now were able to further their existing efforts by modernizing their equipment and technique.

Yet others are large producers who updated their facilities and processes to take advantage of the new conditions, along the way helping to redefine pisco. Santiago Queirolo is the best example: at the turn of the millennium the company completely revamped its operations, planting new vines from France for wine and from Peru for pisco (replacing the *galeras* with the modern T-system of vine growing), and installing a state-of-the-art winery of high tech de-stemmers and presses, and temperature-controlled stainless-steel fermentation tanks with the capacity to produce five million liters of wine a year. The company also invested in a new, computer-regulated alembique made in France.

All this activity triggered something of a boomlet in pisco. Don Amoretti, the alembique-maker, recalls that in 2005 he had one of his busiest years ever, building a dozen handmade alembiques.

The one thing that unites all these producers is an unstinting focus on quality. That means adhering to the denomination rules, of course, but there is more to it: it means extending quality control from the grapes straight through to the bottles.

As the Spanish colonists knew, excellence starts with the vine. Outside Ica today the view is essentially unchanged since the days of the big Jesuit haciendas. Rows of leafy vines held high on the old Spanish galeras or on the more modern, lower T-trellises stretch across the flat valley bottom, right to the edge of the high desert. It's a striking sight: the lush verdure ends abruptly, with immense, lifeless sand dunes rising sharply to toothy black mountains utterly devoid of vegetation.

When Rodrigo Peschiera Mifflin was a kid, his family were cotton growers, part of the cotton boom of the 1970s. "When I saw my first vine, in my grandfather's garden in Chincha," he recalls, "I fell in love with it. When I saw the grapes hanging down from that vine, I said 'this has to be mine.'"

To Peschiera grapes were a lot more interesting than cotton, "With this particular plant, you have to use your hands; you have to use your knowledge; you have to be an artist." So he learned viticulture, eventually traveling to California's Napa Valley to study, where his devotion to the grape only deepened. "The grape is the queen of all the fruits," he declares, "you have so many different varieties and flavors of grapes. You have everything: all colors, all tastes, all textures."

When he returned to Peru 15 years ago, his intention was to help form the basis for fine pisco by growing great grapes. "If you plant the right grape and harvest it at the right time," he says, "you will have a good fermentation and a good distillation, and a great product." It certainly makes sense: one liter of pisco is the distilled essence of seven kilos of grapes—12 kilos if it's mosto verde.

With his father, Peschiera bought an old hacienda called La Caravedo. Set among the vineyards at the edge of Ica's broad valley, it is the oldest documented distillery still operating in the Americas—it has been making pisco since 1684. He remembers that it seemed ancient, "I came from the Napa Valley where everything was stainless steel and high technology, and when I came to this land and this old winery, we didn't have anything modern at all. I was a little discouraged."

"But little by little," he continues, "this history, this land, this environment started talking to me. It told me that I had to take care of that part of the past. So I decided to restore the old buildings, and I started making a style of pisco that they made 325 years ago."

Accordingly, he planted his vines in the traditional style—deep, without grafted rootstocks. "I want to grow a big root system," he says "the root system works together with the soil, which is a living thing, and together they bring flavors into the grapes."

Restoring the old ways also meant farming without modern chemicals. La Caravedo became the only organic vineyard in Peru, but Peschiera went one step further and began farming the land using biodynamic techniques and, as the Jesuits and Incas before, the region's abundant guano for fertilizer.

He says that one of the benefits of farming organically is that it helps promote healthy populations of wild yeast in the vineyards, the yeasts that under the Denomination of Origin are the only allowable fermentation agents. But there's more still: "If you put your best hopes and wishes into the land," he says, "and do the right thing looking at the soil and the moon, doing things at the right time, then you start making a nice, soft, clean wonderful pisco. It's fabulous!"

"It helps the soil, the grapes, the drinkers, and the environment," he says. And it leads to a better pisco because organic grapes naturally contain less copper, which at high levels can create a bitter mineral taste in the pisco.

Although Peschiera sold La Caravedo in 2010, he continues to advocate his brand of organic viticulture and small, hands-on production.

"Our method was techno-artisanal," he says. "La Caravedo was an exclusive boutique producer for the kind of people who like to sip a fine pisco straight." His piscos emphasized the fruitiness inherent in the grapes, and toned down the harsh burn common to higher-alcohol *piscos de los machos*.

In this, Peschiera was flying in the face of the existing domestic market for pisco, yet he quickly developed a following. Under Peschiera, La Caravedo's pisco became very influential, immensely raising the product's profile at home in Peru.

"When you sip a nice pisco," he says, "that means that the people making it did an excellent job in the fields, in the winery, the distillation—everywhere. The pisco world has to do with people who love their soil, people who love their culture."

Peschiera says that the Ica Valley has the ideal *terroir* for pisco grapes. "We are in a tropical latitude," he says, "but we are about 50 kilometers from the ocean and at 400 meters of elevation. This gives us a lot of sunshine, perfect agronomic conditions with cool nights and warm days—desert conditions—to grow grapes with more sugar."

Not only does it never rain, but there is no frost either, and the conditions are very consistent, ensuring predictable harvests year after year. (This lack of rain could be a problem in the future: in spite of controls on new wells, the water table in Ica is dropping and without irrigation everything would be dry and dead in short order.)

Peschiera explains that as the grapes mature in January and February, the sugar levels increase and the acidity decreases—not ideal for winemaking, but perfect for distillation. "You can ferment for five to twelve days, depending on the temperature," he says, "and then right away it goes into the alembique to capture all the flavors that were in the fermentation."

The new breed of pisco-makers place great stock in obtaining just the right grapes. Many producers own their own vineyards, but even those who do not closely monitor the progress of the fruit during the growing season, visiting frequently and making sure that the grapes are developing the sugar levels they desire.

It's also important that the vines be pruned correctly,

since the alembiques have limited capacity and form a bottleneck in the pisco-making process. In August grape growers begin their pruning cycle, cutting back the previous year's growth and encouraging new shoots. But they have to stagger this pruning in order to stretch out the harvest and not overwhelm the bodegas with too many grapes at once.

"You have to be involved months before the harvest," says Cecilia Ledesma, who launched pisco Qollqe in 2008. Ledesma, like many American winemakers, owns neither vines nor bodega. Instead, she takes a contemporary outsourcing approach to creating her ultra-premium pisco, hiring expertise and buying quality. "I am only buying the best grapes," she goes on, "I have to choose very carefully."

With a background as the owner of a cockfighting ring—a sport long associated with pisco—she set out in 2007 with the single-minded goal of making the best pisco possible. She had been married to a pisco-maker, but had never made her own, so she started systematically learning everything she needed to know to maintain the highest standards at every step of the way.

Qollqe, which means "silver" in Quechua, is made from late-harvest grapes, which have more flavor, and is a *mosto yema*—a very rare type of pisco made from the initial stomping of the grapes, without additional mechanical pressing. This makes it delicate and rich, perfectly rounded without any rough or bitter qualities whatsoever.

Ledesma has the time and devotion to guide this process right into the bottle: "I choose the grapes, how the fermentation takes place, when to cut," she says. "At every step, I make the decisions." In these carefully crafted liquors, you can taste the pisco-maker's hand: "My pisco is different from anyone else's," she says, "because it contains my personality. Every pisco is unique."

But this distinctiveness comes at a price: her output is extremely limited—just 4,000 liters last year—and her pisco is one of the most expensive. When you go so far as to cool the fermentation tanks by hand, wrapping them in ice on hot days, there's no way to produce a lot. "Qollqe is heart. It's pure passion," explains Ledesma. "That's why it's not cheap. It can't be."

BIGGER PLAYERS

It may not be cheap, but good pisco does not have to be completely out of reach. While they share a devotion to quality and producing excellent piscos, Viñas de Oro is in every other way the opposite of Ledesma's operation. It is owned by the Brescia Group, a family-held company that is the largest conglomerate in Peru, working in every important sector, from fisheries to mining. Along the coast, its agribusiness subsidiary (farming was the family's original business) owns huge areas of land, growing crops like oranges and avocados for export. Yet the company's first pisco efforts, in 1996, were remarkable for their modest size. "We were at first just playing," says Ricardo Polis, the general manager of Viñas de Oro, "doing a very small amount of pisco only for the family and friends."

But in 2004, encouraged by the rave reviews their pisco was garnering, the company took the plunge and scaled rapidly, building a new, state-of-the art bodega in Chincha. Viñas de Oro (which means "Vines of Gold") quickly became the largest of the premium brands of pisco, and the third largest overall. (Queirolo is the biggest, Biondi is second.)

Viñas de Oro grows pisco grapes on 82 hectares around its bodega. The facility, which opened in 2005, is neat and orderly, in an airy but relatively utilitarian space of concrete floors with a high metal roof. Rows of thousand-liter temperature-controlled stainless-steel tanks—the same ones used all over the world at modern wineries—fill the room. In the back is a row of alembiques—eight 1,000-liter units made by Don Amoretti a few years ago. They are encased in brick, and fired by natural gas. The swan's necks descend into graceful copper coils suspended in giant concrete tanks that are filled with water during distillation.

On the other side of each tank, in a concrete pit below the level of the alembique, is a deceptively modest spigot—the business end of the still, the spring from which gushes forth the *chicharrón*, the fresh pisco. During distillation the place is hectic: the alembiques run 24 hours a day, seven days a week for three or four months, from March to May. Nonetheless, the bodega is so well designed that even at the peak each year it requires just 15 people to run it. The rest of the year there are just three people on site.

Each run takes about eight hours, then the alembique is cleaned out and refreshed with a thousand more liters of fermented mosto. Down in each pit, a highly trained technician must make the call about when to cut the head and the tail. "How to know when to cut it?" asked Magin Sole of Viñas de Oro rhetorically, his dark eyes penetrating and focused. "We measure the specific gravity, and then we taste it. We are looking for a smoky or even burnt flavor —*pulchado*—like an ashtray. That is when you cut it."

It's tough going, hot work with long hours: "From a thousand liters of wine, after eight hours of work," he says, "we can get up to 250 liters of pisco. With mosto verde we can get 150 to 180 liters."

But the pisco still isn't ready to drink when it comes out of the alembique. Under the denomination, it must rest for at least three months. Viñas de Oro lets their pisco age for between eight months and a year. "The aromas and flavors come together," explains Sole. "Other flavors mature, and the alcoholic taste diminishes. Some volatile elements blow off into the air."

If all of this new equipment and advanced technique ensures a consistent—and consistently good—pisco, con-

scientious pisco-makers use it only insofar as it enhances the essence of the product. "The technology has advanced a lot," says Sole. "But what has absolutely not changed is the alembique. It is the same as ever. We have applied technology to the artisanal process. There is much less opportunity for contamination now; it's completely aseptic in the machines. Why use open tinajas, when with this equipment the pisco never comes into contact with the air?"

"It leads to more consistency, a cleaner pisco, much better flavors," he says, leading us into the tasting room, where the entire Viñas de Oro line sat winking at us from behind a dark wood bar. "In the past there wasn't really pisco of such high quality."

"We are the first to apply technology in the production of piscos," he went on while I eyed the bottles. "It's been done for a long time in wine, but not in pisco. The rest are starting to try the same thing now. Eventually they all will be using it. Any that stay behind won't be able to compete in the market."

In the bright yellow tasting room deep inside the high walls of the bodega, I thought of doña Juanita at Tres Generaciones. She has also embraced new ways, yet has retained much more of the ancient, artisanal process, including wood-fired falcas and all-but-forgotten specialty pisco recipes. And she makes incredible pisco too. "The young people today are going crazy with all their technology!"

she had said on that afternoon we met, under the Quebranta arbor next to the falca. I realized the Viñas de Oro bodega had that same smell—of rich, sweet raisins—and noticed that the ground outside the fermentation shed was similarly burgundy colored from the pomace that had been spread on it.

And there was a lot more of it. As conscientious as she is, doña Juanita has pushed the small-batch process as far as it can go: Tres Generaciones makes 50,000 liters of pisco a year, just one-third of Viñas de Oro's annual production. And Viñas de Oro was built with expansion in mind—the bodega is running at just 70 percent of its capacity. If pisco is going to reach a bigger market with a quality product, it will be with large-scale operations like this one.

Viñas de Oro, thanks to its vast landholdings and the ambitious scope of its business, does something no other pisco producer has attempted: the company makes and sells pisco from six of the eight grapes permitted by the denomination. The only one it does not produce, Uvina, is allowed as pisco only when it is grown in the Lunahuana valley near Lima—and there is some debate as to whether it is truly its own variety. Viñas de Oro sells six pisco puros, plus an acholado and several mosto verdes—the largest range of any producer. (The company's production of Mollar is very small and it is not commercialized.) And, like wine, the bottles are labeled with the vintage (in Peru,

anyway; marking the year of production for spirits is illegal in the United States). The 2006 Viñas de Oro Mosto Verde Italia is legendary—people hoard it. You know you're in the inner sanctum of pisco when someone brings out a bottle.

"It's part of our plan to show the world, and the Peruvian consumer, that pisco is not just Quebranta," said Sole, "that there are other varieties and that they make great pisco. We present the consumer with the unique possibility of saying 'my pisco… is this!' They don't have to be stuck with Quebranta."

"Quebranta is so widely grown because it is the variety that gives the best yield. From the same weight of grapes it can produce the most pisco. It's not a question of quality or flavor—it's about the volume."

Even so, the company's three top sellers, by far, are Quebranta, acholado, and Italia (their acholado is made with a Quebranta base blended with Italia and a little Torontel). Ricardo Polis sees it as Viñas de Oro's job to spread the word about the depth of the piscos available. "We need to do more marketing and introduce all the varieties," he says. "We are on the horse and we have to ride it."

OVERCOMING PROBLEMS WITH QUALITY

Together, these new-wave producers comprise an unprecedented boom in pisco. There are 364 bodegas in Peru today that have the Denomination of Origin, and they pro-

OPPOSITE:
top: At Bodega Viñas de Oro a technician monitors fermentation *bottom:* a farmworker gingerly inspects and trims bunches of grapes to achieve optimal flavor.

duced 6.5 million liters in 2008, a stunning increase from just 1.5 million liters in 2002.

But the market is not as organized as it could be. Half the production is gray-market pisco, produced without paying taxes and sold directly from bodegas to consumers and restaurants, mostly in the pisco-producing regions.

Worse, a lot of the production cannot properly be called pisco under the rules of the Denomination of Origin. Some producers actively cheat by adding sugar to the mosto (creating a telltale sardine-like off flavor), or adding cane alcohol to the product. Some add sugar and water to pomace (skins and stems left after pressing) and undertake a second fermentation, creating something more akin to Italian grappa. Some use non-pisco grapes, including discards from table grape exporters. Others quietly dose the mosto with yeast or continue traditional but no longer permitted practices like tossing a mango or a few cherries into the alembique for that little extra flavor dimension.

Theoretically, the governing body of the denomination should put a stop to these practices, but it lacks teeth— or even much of a budget. The National Institute for the Protection of Competition and Intellectual Property (INDE-COPI) is part of the Peruvian Ministry of Agriculture, but it is controlled by pisco-makers. It cannot afford to undertake blind testing using bottles purchased from retail stores, as it should to ensure impartiality. Instead, bodegas submit their own samples to the authority.

Ricardo Polis estimates that, with high technology and big economies of scale, the lower end for a retail bottle of real, scrupulously legal pisco in a Peruvian supermarket should be about 35 soles (in 2010 there were roughly three soles to the US dollar). A 750 ml bottle of Viñas de Oro Quebranta sells for about 65 soles, while the cheapest liquor sold as pisco on the market retails at around 19 soles.

Polis believes a shakeout is coming. "The number of brands now is unsustainable," he says. "A lot of them are going to die out." And if governing bodies aren't up to undertaking the cull, it is the market power of educated consumers that is going to do the job.

A sophisticated scene of pisco-drinkers is re-emerging, especially in Lima, where fine novo-Andino gastronomy has now become a part of the social fabric of the city's middle class. And some of the most vocal proponents for quality pisco are the professional tasters who have emerged with a focus on pisco.

Lucero Villagarcía de Bedoya began her career as a sommelier, but fell in love with pisco. "I really like wine," she told me, "but when I discovered pisco it was like something greater than me, something I had to devote myself to." As the founder of the Association of Independent Pisco Tasters, she is an enthusiastic advocate for quality pisco, but also a righteous crusader against the bad stuff.

"I love the good piscos," she told me one night at a Lima restaurant that specializes in refined versions of dishes from Northern Peru. "A good pisco is marvelous, marvelous, marvelous! It's a pleasure! There's no comparison with a good pisco!" During the course of the meal, she kept reaching into her bag and pulling out samples for me to taste—and not just the good stuff.

"This one— *¡malo!*" she said, nearly spitting in disgust. Villagarcía and her panel of tasters buy samples of pisco from stores and then taste them blind. "*Copa una— ¡blech! Copa dos—¡mmm! Copa tres—¡euww!*" she mimed. "At the end, we find out what they are. So we have data: 60 percent of piscos in Peru are bad."

This kind of forthrightness is lamentably rare in Peru. "I am not a producer or a commercializer," she emphasizes. "I'm totally independent. If I say it's good or bad, it's based on my technical organoleptic assessment. I became an expert by tasting, tasting, tasting, tasting, tasting! I taste pisco every day of the week—I know what is good and what is bad."

Villagarcía has made it her life's mission to improve pisco by calling out poor quality. "I suffer when I see bad stuff on the shelves!" she says. "I would rather people drink good Chilean pisco than bad Peruvian pisco," she adds blasphemously, passing me a bottle of Chilean aguardiente she had smuggled into Peru. "I am the pisco subversive! The pisco terrorist! People want to kill me but I don't care!"

She tips her head back and laughs merrily.

A measure of just how bad things got during the dark days is one of Viñas de Oro's messages to Peruvian drinkers: that now they can drink pisco without worrying how they will feel the next day. "A lot of people are afraid of pisco," Ricardo Polis told me in yet another outstanding Lima restaurant, over a chilcano made with Viñas de Oro Quebranta. "In my generation—I am almost fifty—we don't drink pisco; we drink whiskey, rum, and vodka. My father drank pisco."

"We need these objective professional tasters," says Soledad Marroquín, a journalist and a taster herself. She says that broadening pisco's appeal will also require more careful market research than has been done in the past. "We don't have any real market data that the producers can use," she says. "What do people prefer? Quebranta? Torontel? Foreigners really like the aromatics. Europeans love it when they come here, but they don't find Quebranta appealing—yet that's what we make."

But Marroquín recognizes that the approach of the devoted purists will not work for everyone. "We're such hardliners," she says. "We say 'you have to drink it straight! It's a crime to put it in a cocktail!'—but the youth aren't going to drink it straight. If you're twenty years old in Peru, you drink beer or rum and coke. I feel personally that we are missing the youth; pisco is mostly drunk by people over forty."

COCKTAILS MAKE A COMEBACK

That's where Omar Cosio comes in. As the Brand Manager for Viñas de Oro, he's been thinking a lot about Chilcanos. Simply a mix of ginger ale and pisco, usually Quebranta, with a little lime and maybe some bitters, the Chilcano is the pisco marketer's dream. It is clean, refreshing, and easy to make. And unlike a Pisco Sour, anyone can make one at home. Also unlike its more popular cousin, a Chilcano allows the quality of the pisco and even the grape varietal flavors to shine through. It's also faster to make and more profitable for restaurants and bars. Plus, it's more versatile: a Chilcano can be enjoyed poolside, as an aperitif, or even with food.

If Cosio has an uphill climb—he says 75 percent of pisco is consumed in pisco sours—he believes the young are open to his message. In Peru, college students drink beer and rum, but once they get out of school and get jobs in the booming economy, they start going out to restaurants and bars—and trying Chilcanos. "Then people get into the question of what kind of pisco they like," he says. "In a Chilcano you can recognize the quality of the pisco. You can taste it."

Cosio's approach has been to target the hip and high-end spots in Lima, the flagships of the upswing in pisco consumption, where inspired barmen serve up inventive concoctions to eager, discerning customers.

The Huaringas Bar at the Brujas de Cachiche restau-rant was, in 2001, the first to take the Pisco Sour in a new direction, adding other fruits from Peru's astounding cornucopia. The place, in an old mansion, rambling across several floors inside and outside the building, became known for its Maracuyá (Passion Fruit) Sour.

"The fruits you add to a sour have to be acidic, like lime," says Maria del Rosario Alcorta, the owner of the bar. A trained chef, she brings a culinary sensibility to her drinks menu. It's certainly struck a chord among Limeños—Rosario estimates Huaringas sells 1,300 liters of pisco a month.

While the Huaringas Bar was the first to expand the world of sours, Ayahuasca, also in a magnificent old mansion, has taken it the farthest. The bar is in Barranco, a graceful tree-lined town full of 100-year-old mansions right at the edge of the Pacific. Once a country escape for Lima's elite, Barranco has been enveloped by the city's sprawl, but it remains a distinctively charming enclave.

At Ayahuasca, which opened in 2008, the fruit sour concept has been extended to a dozen or more Peruvian fruits that bartenders crank out to a constant din of blenders. Part bar, part nightclub, it's packed with those elusive young professionals—all of them drinking pisco. "This is a renaissance," says Raúl Diez Canseco, one of the owners. "We are beginning to develop our own nationalism and to be proud of what we produce here."

While these spots appeal to the young, and have

OPPOSITE:
top: Soledad Marroquin, journalist and expert pisco taster; *middle:* Omar Cosio, brand manager for Viñas de Oro and evangelist for the Chilcano; *bottom:* Maria del Rosario Alcorta, owner of the very popular Huaringas Bar in Lima.

greatly broadened the appeal of pisco in that demographic, even more interesting, more refined pisco drinks are appearing elsewhere in Lima.

Malabar is a stylish lounge of a restaurant partly owned by José Antonio Schiaffino, or "Chafi," as everyone in pisco calls him. An amiable character of longstanding bonhomie, Chafi was involved in Lima's first surfing scene on Waikiki Beach in Miraflores (the surfing club there is one of the oldest in the Americas).

An avid collector of "things," Chafi's house is filled with obsessively gleaned bric-a-brac: antique Polynesian totems; turn-of-the-century glass paperweights; ancient Coca-Cola bottles. He keeps much of his collection of old glassware (which includes everything from antique glass made for the Spanish Royal family to Las Vegas shot glasses) in display cases at Malabar.

Fortunately for pisco lovers, one of Chafi's obsessions is cocktail history, with a focus on pisco. He has published a series on historic pisco cocktails and has done much to revive old-school drinks like the Capitán.

At Malabar, the barmen have taken these classic sensibilities and broadened them to a new breed of pisco cocktails. Making use of the latest fine piscos, house-made macerados, and fresh, ripe fruits, they turn out marvelously balanced, nuanced drinks that exploit pisco's best features.

Barman Jesús Ávila Sovero's Zing, for example, combines Quebranta with lime, house-made ginger syrup, and bitters to create a deeply quenching, clean cocktail that riffs off the Chilcano.

This kind of mixology is being diligently explored at Mayta, a swank bar and restaurant on the edge of Barranco that opened in 2009. There, chef Jaime Pesaque Roose makes macerados both traditional and wildly creative. He combs Peru, particularly the area around his jungle hometown in the north, to find an edenic bounty of botanicals. (His inventive menu also makes prominent use of Amazonian ingredients.)

Back in Lima, he figures out the best way to use each ingredient. Making macerados is not just a matter of dumping a bunch of herbs into a jug of pisco: the time, temperature, number of infusions, and action of any additional ingredients all determine the outcome.

Pesaque takes the time to get it right. He has more than 30 macerados on the menu, and is aiming to have 50. He prefers to serve these drinks as variations on the chilcano, taking advantage of that drink's basic simplicity to let the macerados shine.

"We are looking for rare things," he says. "In-season fruits, herbs, spices. We take trips around the forest and get *zapote mamey, chuchuhuasi, taperiba,* and the results are surprising because the fruits mix very well with ginger

ale and result in these different Chilcanos."

At the edge of Miraflores and Barranco, a precipitous cliff plunges towards the ocean. Down there, on pilings over the surf, is perhaps the best place in Lima to try the new breed of pisco cocktails. At Cala, a restaurant and bar with glass walls looking out to sea, and a patio suspended just above the water, Enrique Vidarte Morales may be the world's most inspired new-school pisco mixologist.

A veteran barman—he worked at Gastón Acurio's flagship restaurant Astrid y Gastón—Vidarte brought nearly three decades of experience to Cala when he started there in 2007. Backed by a superb collection of the best piscos, Vidarte specializes in creating cocktails centering around the aromatic pisco varieties.

"Each type of pisco has its own character," he says, gesturing at the rows of clear bottles behind the bar. "I try to find the right one to balance the other ingredients. For example, if I am making a berry cocktail, I use an aromatic pisco that complements the fruit flavors." With that he begins mixing, talking all the while. "You have to find the ingredients—pisco, cream, fruit, whatever—of the highest quality, and blend it with a balanced flavor: acid, bitter, sweet, and so on."

The result in this case was a Key Lime Pisco, a blended drink presented as a mound of soft green lime sorbet sitting in a lake of mosto verde Quebranta. It was sublime: cool and sharp, perfectly balanced and beautifully presented—one of the most imaginative cocktails any of us had ever tried.

Vidarte says that more people are starting to specify the pisco that they want in their drinks, and that people are even rediscovering the pleasures of pisco puro. "It used to be that the people who like pisco puro were the old people," he said, pouring a glass for us to try. "But now all the public is getting into it—women, too. Women like mosto verde; it's smoother. Men will drink anything."

This is music to Lucero Villagarcía's ears. "I tell people: quality is up to you. When you are out and you ask for a drink, ask what pisco they have. Order it by name!"

As pisco enters a second golden age, part of its strength lies in maintaining its historical roots even as it evolves. And those roots are being lovingly tended at the Bar Inglés at the Hotel Country Club.

That bar, which signaled a shift in Lima's social life away from the center and out towards San Isidro and Miraflores in the mid-twentieth century, is now headed by Roberto Melendez de la Cruz, universally known as the finest hand when it comes to the classic pisco cocktails.

Even his Pisco Sour is a revelation. He makes it in the old style—with good pisco, of course, but also different ratios of ingredients that allow the pisco to come through the lime and sugar. And there's good reason: his father learned to make Pisco Sours at the Hotel Maury in 1946 before moving on to the Hotel Bolívar. So Melendez received the

OPPOSITE: Some of the macerados at Lima's Mayta bar and restaurant.

transmission directly from Victor Morris and Mario Bruiget. Like the greats of olden days, he started working as a bar back for his father when he was just 15 years old.

"My father always said, to be a *coctelero* you have to start with a good Pisco Sour," he explained, as he held up a full shaker and let loose the music of ice and liquor inside the quiet, wood-paneled Bar Inglés.

He poured it out, a light green elixir with a thin cap of foam on top—thinner than the frothy modern style. Then he added three drops of bitters—they are for aroma only, to be smelled but not tasted as they float on their cloud of meringue.

"Pisco Sour is an aperitif," he said, placing the glass in front of me, "so it has to stimulate the appetite. It has to be dry; to do that you have to use grapes with less aroma,

in this case Quebranta. We use four ounces of Quebranta with one ounce of fresh lime juice, one ounce of simple syrup, a quarter of an egg white, ice, and shake in a cocktail shaker for eight to ten seconds, and strain into a chilled glass, so there is no change in temperature."

"That is the traditional recipe, before the cocktail got sweeter and became like a candy in which you couldn't taste the pisco any more."

"These cocktails are part of our patrimony," he added, watching me taste the Pisco Sour. "We wanted to do it right—10 years ago there was nothing like this. When I started working at this hotel, we sold whiskey most of all, then vodka, and then pisco followed by gin and rum and all the others. Now, the liquor that is most ordered here is pisco."

OPPOSITE:
top left: Timothy Childs at the Country Club's Bar Inglés; *top middle:* Enrique Vidarte at Cala making his one-of-a-kind cocktails; *right:* Enrique Vidarte's astounding Key Lime Pisco cocktail; *bottom left:* Roberto Melendez de la Cruz of Bar Inglés serving a Pisco Punch; *bottom middle:* Friends toasting with macerado-based Chilcanos at Mayta.

7

On Cherub's Wings
Pisco Returns to America

"The first confrontation I had about the nationality of pisco was with my grandmother," says Guill-ermo Toro-Lira. A Peruvian electrical engineer who has lived in the San Francisco Bay Area for de-cades, Toro-Lira is a great lover of pisco, and so was his grandmother—but she was Chilean. "She came to live with us in Lima," he remembers, "She liked to play the guitar, to write songs. And she loved pisco."

It was only towards the end of her life that she admitted to Toro-Lira that perhaps pisco had been invented in Peru after all. She said that her Peruvian friends had finally convinced her.

But Toro-Lira was troubled, "The Chileans are so strong in their conviction that every Peru-vian has in the back of their mind a little bit of doubt—maybe pisco *was* Chilean. There's a small possibility, no?"

So in the late 1990s he set out to discover the truth, "The whole time I had been in San Fran-cisco," he says, "I noticed there was a Peruvian presence in California history—Domingo Ghirardelli, James Lick, and others—but nobody had explored it, either here or in Peru. Nobody had a clue."

Before long, he found what he was looking for, a written reference to pisco being imported to San Francisco from Peru aboard an English ship in 1839. "I said, 'Aha! Pisco's Peruvian!'" he remembers, still elated by the discovery. "I double-checked, looking for mentions of pisco from Chile—there were plenty of Chileans here, too—and there was nothing. Zero. Nothing."

"Oh wow, I thought. This was the first time there's evidence by a third party independent of Peru and Chile—which are completely biased of course. I felt like I had settled this business."

Toro-Lira may have quieted his nagging doubts, but he had also unwittingly stumbled into a whole new field of research. On a visit to a public library, he found the complete set of bulletins of the California Historical Society, occupying 20 feet of shelf space. He asked Brenda, his wife and tireless assistant, to scan the entire series, looking for mentions of pisco.

After two hours, Brenda hit pay dirt, a 1973 article called "Secrets of the Pisco Punch Revealed." So they went home and tried the recipe. "People loved it," Toro-Lira recalls, "but something was not right. It did not match the historical descriptions written by people who had tasted Duncan Nicol's Pisco Punch."

And so began Toro-Lira's saga of investigation into the notorious cocktail. Doggedly conducting research in San Francisco, Panama, and Peru, applying the exacting standards of his engineering background, he set his sights on uncovering Duncan Nicol's lost recipe.

When Nicol died in 1926, he took the secret of Pisco Punch to his grave. Nobody had known the recipe even while he was alive; only his deaf mute assistant ever saw him make it. But plenty of people had tasted it, and had described its flavor and effects in detail.

After years of research, along the way discovering far more of the history of the Bank Exchange and pisco in general than had been known previously, (among other things, he discovered the 82-page guestbook from Morris' Bar in Lima and painstakingly cross-referenced it with city directories and other sources). Toro-Lira came up with a recipe of staggering complexity—and staggering historical depth.

In Toro-Lira's estimation, Duncan Nicol's Pisco Punch included pisco, obviously—Italia, probably mosto verde—but also a suite of other ingredients that were rare and very expensive in San Francisco a hundred years ago, as befits a drink for which Nicol charged between 25 and 50 cents. There was gum arabic, the sap of an African acacia; Acapulco limes, the big seedless green ones; and Cayenne pineapple grown in Hawaii (even the peel was used as a flavoring agent, the way the Peruvian nonalcoholic drink *chicha morada* is flavored with pineapple rind). The recipe takes a day to make, and it is delicious.

"The combination with the pineapple is magic done in heaven," says Toro-Lira. "Duncan Nicol—or whoever was the first to mix pineapple with Italia—that guy is a genius."

But it still wasn't quite right. Most glaringly, Toro-Lira couldn't get any Italia in San Francisco. In fact, he could barely get any pisco at all. In 2001, the only Peruvian pisco he could find in the Bay Area was at the large beverage chain BevMo!—and they had just one bottle. When he wanted to have a party to unveil his elaborate historical Pisco Punch recipe, Toro-Lira had to drive all over the region, raiding all the BevMo!s until he had amassed nine undistinguished bottles.

AMERICAN PISCO PIONEERS

Fortunately, a few years later, a decade into the pisco renaissance in Peru, more brands started to appear in the United States. Chief among them was BarSol, created by Diego Loret de Mola, a Peruvian living in New Jersey. To that point, all pisco imported to the United States had been aimed at communities of Peruvians living abroad, but Loret de Mola had a different idea.

Rather than market to Peruvians, he was going after bartenders, high-end mixologists in particular. "They are the gatekeepers of the experience," he says.

It was a modest start. After developing the plan for five years, and buying a bodega in 2004, Loret de Mola brought a single 20-foot container of Quebranta to the United States in 2005—just 140 cases. As a measure of how inward looking the Peruvian pisco scene was, that container made a splash in Peru. "It was big news," he says. "'Oh my God! A container of pisco has been exported!'" Even three years later, in 2008, 95 percent of the pisco produced in Peru was consumed there. "We were immediately the biggest exporter that year," he recalls, "it was a wake-up call to the older producers."

Loret de Mola has been the most important promoter of pisco among American mixologists. He leads small tours of influential members of the sector to Peru's pisco-producing regions. The tours are comprehensive—and a lot of fun. I tagged along one day in Lima when he took a group to the English Cemetery in Callao, so we could toast Victor Morris' headstone with a Pisco Sour. (Naturally we poured out a bit for the old fellow to enjoy as well.)

The commitment of the new breed of pisco exporters is remarkable. "I have wanted to do this since I was 12 years old," says Melanie da Trindade-Asher, the founder of Macchu Pisco. That was how old she was when she moved with her family from Peru to the United States. In 2003, fresh from Harvard Business School, her dream came true when she launched her company with her sister Lizzie and their mother.

Their production is nothing short of obsessive: while

> Finally, after years of painstaking research hunting the globe for the original Pisco Punch recipe, author Guillermo Toro-Lira has deduced the missing ingredient….

the mosto is fermenting, nobody is allowed to raise their voices near the tanks; classical music is piped in to soothe the yeast. "Yeast is a living thing," explains Melanie da Trindade-Asher. "You have to treat it well." For their Ñusta mosto verde, the sisters use low temperature fermentation in chilled tanks over just one and a half days to cram an entire 16 kilos of fruit into a single liter of pisco. No wonder they produce only 100 bottles of it a year!

By 2007, the combined exports of the company's Macchu Pisco (a Quebranta), La Diablada (an acholado), and Ñusta made the da Trindade-Ashers the largest exporters of pisco from Peru. "The growth has been wonderful," Melanie says. "We hand deliver the product, basically. We are the two girls who carry pisco around in Gucci bags."

"It's a labor of love," says Lizzie da Trindade-Asher, who leads the company's marketing efforts in the United States. "It's a cause: even before I tell people about our brand, I have to tell them about pisco: pisco, pisco, pisco, pisco!"

The story of pisco has natural interest for mixologists, particularly those interested in Latin America or historical cocktails. When James Schenk, a San Francisco restaurateur whose mother is Peruvian and who went to culinary school in Peru, opened his pan-Latin restaurant Destino in San Francisco in 2000, he carried only three piscos—and two of them were Chilean. "It was honestly just hard to get," he says. "No one even knew what pisco was."

But Schenk was committed to the liquor nonetheless: "One of the great things that sets pisco apart is that once you try it it's easy to get addicted to it; it's easy to sell," he says. "The different levels of aromatics you get, and all the varietals too, make it a lot more compelling than vodka; it tells a lot more of a story than gin."

THE SECRET INGREDIENT

In 2005, just as he was thinking of expanding his restaurant to include a bar, Schenk met Guillermo Toro-Lira. As if by magic, a space became available right next door to the restaurant, and the pair opened Pisco Latin Lounge in 2008. It was the first pisco bar in the United States in the modern era.

It is also the only place in the world to try the elaborate historically accurate Pisco Punch recipe that Toro-Lira had reconstructed. Ever the engineer, Toro-Lira has systematized its preparation, and has even invented special equipment: his "Pisco Transfuser" is a precisely machined device of tubing, syringes, and mean-looking spikes that looks like a high-tech device for torturing pineapples. Cubes of pineapple are laid in a tray, the lid is closed, and pisco is injected into the heart of each one.

Toro-Lira says he has developed other innovations as well, but true to the history of secrecy that Duncan Nicol and others maintained when it comes to pisco, he will not divulge them—not even to his business partner.

What he will talk about is the missing secret ingredient from the original recipe. Based on the published writings about Nicol's punch, Toro-Lira had solved many of the drink's mysteries—the gum arabic, for example. Because it coats the tongue and blocks the taste of alcohol, it accounted for the observation that Pisco Punch goes down like lemonade, but packs a wallop.

But there was more to it than that. Contemporary accounts had described the drink as "floating the drinker in the region of bliss of hasheesh and absinthe," and possessing such emboldening properties that "it will make a gnat fight an elephant." Many accounts of drinks taken at the Bank Exchange, including Rudyard Kipling's, mention a feeling of flight. Notwithstanding traditional pisco-makers' claims for their liquor, was there something else in Duncan Nicol's Pisco Punch?

"It had to be cocaine," says Toro-Lira.

In the late nineteenth century, cocaine, yet another Peruvian botanical product, was widely available in the United States. Most famously it was in the original recipe of Coca-Cola, but it also appeared in aperitifs like Vin Mariani, in pure solutions available at pharmacies, and in remedies

for everything from toothaches to simple tiredness.

It worked really well—perhaps too well. In 1907, cocaine was banned in the United States. "But Duncan Nicol kept making his drink the same way," says Toro-Lira. "That's why it was a secret recipe—he didn't want it exposed. I don't know what form of cocaine he used—it could have been something like Vin Mariani, or it could have been infused in the pineapple—but I am 99.9 percent sure he used cocaine."

THE NEW WAVE BREAKS ON AMERICAN SHORES

Since that ingredient is not returning to above-board use any time soon, aficionados of historical cocktails can take comfort in the fact that at least the pisco supply in the United States is catching up with them.

A new wave of Peruvian exporters who are connected to the pisco renaissance added to a cohort of American importers in tune with mixology's faithfulness to the classics has vastly improved the pisco situation in this country.

In 2008 Guillermo Ferreyros, a boutique pisco producer, entered the American market with Pisco 100, a high-end acholado. In a departure from the practice of the inwardly focused pisco sector, Ferreyros had from the start intended to export his pisco, so it was designed specifically for the US market. "If you're going to go abroad, you have to go premium," he says.

But it was only because of the force of his vision that he was able to do so. Not a pisco-maker himself, Ferreyros hired his expertise from a sector used to cutting corners. "Convincing the people I was working with that I wanted to go with quality, not quantity, was the hardest thing," he recalls. "It's this attitude that has prevented pisco from succeeding abroad."

Duggan McDonnell is doing much the same thing, but with a twist: he comes to pisco as a mixologist. In 2007 he opened Cantina, a San Francisco bar that, like James Schenk's spots, is focused on Latin America.

"I had a solid background in agave and cane," he says, referring to tequila and rum, "but not grape. There was a hole. I couldn't do a holistic program."

Still, McDonnell, who had never been to Peru at that point, is not the kind of man to let that sort of detail stand in his way. "We opened Cantina with a Pisco Punch as our lead cocktail," he remembers, "even though we had never tasted one—nobody was making them then."

McDonnell quickly became enthusiastic about pisco as a cocktail base, "But," he remembers, "I was always dissatisfied with what I was tasting on the market."

In 2008 Carlos Romero, a Peruvian distiller with a deep background in pisco, approached McDonnell about working together to create a pisco brand aimed at mixologists, one that tapped into the long history between Peru and San Francisco. "I was determined that it had to be a palate-driven pisco," says McDonnell.

In 2010, they, along with partner Walter Moore, released Campo de Encanto, an acholado designed specifically for the historically minded mixologist. Its label features a photo of the House of Pisco, a long-gone post-Prohibition bar in San Francisco's North Beach. (According to a 1957 article in *Gourmet* magazine that also noted the utter impossibility of finding pisco in the United States, the House of Pisco had "served a not un-refreshing arrangement, which the management maintained was the True Sacrament as first devised by Nicol...The drink wasn't a bad one, and contained pineapple juice, and what passed in those days for pisco, but it embodied none of the magical qualities associated with the legend of the Bank Exchange, and a few of them served to induce torpor without exaltation, something like the effect of a slug at the base of the neck.")

By 2010 the pisco scene in America was becoming very interesting indeed. Timothy Childs, another San Franciscan known for his skills at tastemaking and trend-spotting, had just entered the sector. As the founder of TCHO, a highly regarded new-wave chocolate-maker, Childs had been traveling frequently to Peru to buy cacao beans. While there, he couldn't help but try pisco. "It was unlike any alcoholic beverage I had ever had," he says. "I fell in love with it. And I knew it was going to be huge in the States."

OPPOSITE: *top:* Tequila and Pisco champion Enrique Sanchez, head mixologist at La Mar in San Francisco; *middle:* Duggan McDonnell and Timothy Childs testing some of the recipes for this book at San Francisco's Cantina. Also pictured, book designer Tom Ingalls; *bottom:* Duggan McDonnell with mentor Rodolfo Mejía ("La Leyenda") and partner distiller, Carlos Romero, at Bodega Mejía.

Childs, who had trained as a bartender at San Francisco's influential Zuni Café, and remembers having to sneak bottles of quality tequila into restaurants when nobody had ever heard of it, immediately decided to find out more. "I've always had a fascination with flavor and how flavor works," he says, "that's what led me to Peru in the first place."

During one trip, he noticed Viñas de Oro's bodega in Chincha from the road, so he dropped in for a visit. "We got in there," he says, "and I thought 'holy smokes, these guys are serious!'" The timing was perfect. It had been Viñas de Oro's plan from the start to market its pisco both in Peru and abroad.

And the rest is history. Childs, along with his partner Shelley Alger, set up ClearGrape, an importer devoted to fine piscos. Within six months, ClearGrape was putting Viñas de Oro's full line (known as ORO) on shelves in California, and causing a splash among bartenders who could finally get their hands on aromatics and mosto verdes.

As in Peru a few years previously, it marked the return of the full range of varietals. Particularly exciting to San Francisco mixologists is Viñas de Oro's Italia. "It's the first time I've been able to get Italia in the United States," says Guillermo Toro-Lira. Meanwhile, ClearGrape was expanding, developing its own versatile acholado brand, CODE, and importing limited-run high-end boutique piscos.

NEW DRINKERS

For James Schenk, this wave of new piscos has enabled Pisco Latin Lounge to start to live up to his vision. In 2010, the bar carried 38 piscos, all of them Peruvian. Currently it carries the biggest selection of pisco in the country, yet Schenk cautions that, outside of ORO, "the aromatics are still very difficult to get; same story with the mosto verdes." Even so, the bar can treat customers to pisco flights, in turn piquing their interest in going deeper. "Tasting is the best form of education we can do," says Schenk. "It's just starting but that is the future of pisco."

Unlike in Peru, where an older generation has bad memories from the years of pisco purgatory, the emerging pisco market in the United States is, as far as today's drinkers are concerned, completely new. It's growing most among younger, adventurous drinkers. "It's people aged 21 to 39," says Diego Loret de Mola. "They are learning about the cocktail revolution. They want to go out. They want to be seen and they want to see something new and they want to be discovered, and they want to discover something new."

Enrique Sánchez has seen it before. As a bartender for several specialty tequila–focused bars and restaurants in San Francisco at the start of the millennium, he watched that spirit's appeal broaden until it became a staple behind bars throughout the United States. Now, as head bartender for Gastón Acurio's La Mar in San Francisco, he's

hoping pisco is next.

"10 years ago nobody knew what pisco was," he says. "In the past 10 years, bartenders here have been paying more attention to the history of spirits in general, and pisco has snuck into the same movement. It's growing again in San Francisco."

As a Peruvian, Sánchez finds this gratifying. As a bartender, he finds it liberating. "Pisco is a clean, pure spirit," he says. "It's very, very subtle. You can drink it like a Martini or a Manhattan, but it really needs flavors to balance it out. It mixes perfectly with a lot of tropical flavors, like passion fruit or kiwi."

"And it's not even mixed with water, so hangovers don't happen," he says, echoing a common Peruvian sentiment.

(My own experiments have been equivocal. Apparently the trick is to drink only high-end pisco puro when trying the hangover test—it seems like a couple of sours did me in).

The new interest in pisco is growing the entire category across the board. Loret de Mola's BarSol, the first of this new wave of export piscos, has thrived as well as any. "Our volume has done very, very well," he says. "In 2009 we closed with between 4,000 and 5,000 cases. It's still not a lot compared to other products, but we're growing exponentially."

PURE AUDACITY

And it's just the beginning. The most recent pisco to be imported is also the most ambitious new brand of pisco that has ever been conceived. Johnny Schuler is a fixture in Peru. A restaurateur and pisco aficionado (he has written books about it and hosts popular TV programs on the subject), he is a highly regarded social gadfly and charming bon vivant.

He says that for 20 years people have been approaching him to be a partner in pisco businesses. Finally, in 2010, with an American partner, he launched Pisco Portón, and his ambition for the venture is breathtaking. In his first year, he plans to release a million liters, which would account for one-sixth of the entire production of pisco in Peru—and all of it will be for export. Pisco Portón is a mosto verde acholado, meaning that it will probably consume something like one-third of all the pisco grapes in the country.

And that's only the beginning. "I am aiming for a million cases by 2015," says Schuler. "That's triple Peru's entire production today."

Understandably, Pisco Portón has rocked the pisco world in Peru. Grape prices have skyrocketed, and plantings have accelerated (it takes three years for new plantings to come online). Schuler says part of his mission is to undo the land reforms of the 1960s that sent the sector into a tailspin. In the process, he says, he is going to bring about a shakeout. "If you have your own grapes then you can control your costs," he says. "Those who will complain are the opportunists who don't have land, who are producing pisco today because it's a fad. They will be wiped out of the market. Too bad."

Pisco Portón is based at La Caravedo, formerly Rodrigo Peschiera's family's vineyard and the oldest continuously operating bodega in the Americas (although it is no longer managed organically). Pisco Portón is named after the imposing gateway that guards the entrance to the vineyard. Schuler is building a magnificent new distillery and restaurant there, set among the green vines that stretch to the moonscape of dunes and mountains outside the Ica Valley.

His audacity is not without generosity. "It depends on a huge growth in the category," he said over lunch at a clubby restaurant he owns in Lima. "It will force out the ones that are not good, but we will carry on our shoulders a lot of the good producers, because this will open the market for ultra-premium piscos. Five, six, seven others, they're all going to climb on top of my shoulders—the market I open is open for everybody."

It's too early to tell how Pisco Portón is going to affect the market in the United States, but the tens of millions the company plans to spend is sure to raise the profile of the liquor. "We are going to spend more in promotion of Pisco Portón than Peru has spent in the last 150 years on promoting pisco," Schuler says. If he's right, it will thoroughly transform Peruvian pisco and launch it, yet again, in a new direction. But as always, pisco's appeal, and its success, will be based on four hundred years of tradition.

"I am convinced pisco is the best distilled spirit made from wine in the world," Schuler says. "The world of pisco is as fascinating as the world of wine. It's more complex than the world of cognac, Armagnac, or grappa. We have five regions, 42 valleys, eight different grapes, 500 producers. Put all that into an equation and see how many different piscos you have. Each bottle is a world in itself."

OPPOSITE: Peruvian pisco icon and celebrity Johnny Schuler of Pisco Portón, in his restaurant in Lima.

8

Drinking

If you're like me, you must be ready for a drink. This chapter is here to help. As I'm sure you know by now, your enjoyment of your pisco experience depends in large part on drinking the best pisco. If your pisco isn't palatable straight up (or *puro*, as they say in Peru), then how can you expect to make a great-tasting cocktail out of it?

TASTING PISCO PURO

While enjoying a glass of pisco puro is as simple as taking a sip, here's how the professionals do it: First, get the right glassware. In Peru, pisco puro aficionados favor a special pisco glass, a small stemmed glass with a bulb that narrows to a flute. If you aren't lucky enough to have one on hand, look for a small cordial glass. Even a sherry glass will do.

Pour yourself about an ounce. Look at the clear, viscous liquid: it should be free of any color whatsoever and, when you swirl it, it should coat the glass and fall back in thick legs.

Take a gentle whiff. Then do it again, one nostril at a time—you'll find the experiences subtly different. Then give the glass a swirl and sniff again.

Now it's time to taste the "attack." Take a small sip, and hold it in your mouth. Spread it around in your mouth. (Gracefully, please—this isn't mouthwash!)

Swallow, then exhale through your nose, noting the scent as well as the taste. Notice the aromas and flavors: think about on which part of your tongue you feel them as you sip, as you swallow, and as you exhale.

Think about what you taste. Does it remind you of ripe fruit? What kind? Spices? Earth?

Don't get too wrapped up in describing your experience—you taste what you taste, and you enjoy what you enjoy. As professional pisco taster Lucero Villagarcía de Bedoya divulges, "The old-time *pisqueros* make fun of us," and she puts on a mocking voice, "Oh! I taste citrus! I taste flowers!"

As one of those old-time pisqueros, Juanita Martínez de Gonzales at Tres Generaciones puts it succinctly: "These people come and they try the pisco; they say it smells of bananas, and it tastes of apples. It's like saying a chicken soup tastes like fish!"

"I say 'No!'" and she holds her glass up, the Quebranta leaves from the arbor above playing in the lens of clear liquor, "Pisco tastes like grapes!"

VARIETALS AT
A GLANCE

AROMATICS

ITALIA

TORONTEL

ALBILLA

MOSCATEL

BLENDED
ACHOLADO

NON-AROMATICS

QUEBRANTA

NEGRA CRIOLLA

UVINA

MOLLAR

PISCO FLAVOR PROFILES

	GRAPE VARIETY	FLAVOR PROFILE	COCKTAIL SUGGESTIONS
AROMATICS	**Italia**	NOSE: bright citrus and sweet flower TASTE: fragrant orange and lemon blossom, with whispers of honeysuckle and jasmine that stay through the finish	Pisco Punch · Piscotini de Mora · Santa Rosa · Peruvian 75 · Tumbao · Naked Dog · Apple Chilcano · Blackberry Piscotini
	Torontel	NOSE: juicy grape TASTE: strong floral bouquet (rose, gardenia, violet), grape FINISH: lingering floral notes; great velvety texture	Improved Martinez · Torontel Mojito · Flor de Lima · Firecracker Cocktail · Orange Flyer · Strawberry Pisco Collins
	Albilla	NOSE: sweet and subtle melon TASTE: cucumber with a suggestion of melon FINISH: lingering banana and herbal quality	Albilla Sour · Good with most drinks that use Italia or Torontel.
	Moscatel	NOSE: light honey TASTE: cantaloupe, grapes, and Bartlett pear FINISH: bright lemon evolving to a soft vanilla	Peruvian Sparkle · Good with any drinks that use Torontel.
NON-AROMATICS	**Quebranta**	NOSE: subtle aroma of roasted nuts and peat TASTE: toasted almonds and pecans FINISH: tequila-like structure	Chilcano · Pisco Sour · Peruvian Patada · Bee's Sip · Maytini · Key Lime Pisco · Guenaso · Capitán · Viejo · Maracuyá Sour. Can replace tequila in many drinks.
	Negra Criolla	NOSE: aromas of cherry and spice TASTE: dried plums, fresh cherries, with hints of almonds FINISH: reminiscent of orange marmalade	Viejo · Royal Peruvian Sidecar · Peach Sour
	Uvina	NOSE: olive oil, hay, and mango TASTE: olive oil, mango, hay and banana	Uvina Martini
	Mollar	NOSE: apple, fresh herbs and honey TASTE: apple compote, peach and honey	Strawberry Martini · Pomegranate Martini
BLENDED	**Acholado* (blend)**	NOSE: spice and pine TASTE: orange blossom with hints of fruit FINISH: expansive, subtly sweet and clean	Improved Martinez · Saxon · Ladies Man · Ginger-Maté Pisco Punch · Cholopolitan · Scarlet Fire · Piscola · Este Gabacho · Presidio Punch · Sparkling Ruby. Can replace vodka in many drinks.

"Every drop of pisco is unique," says Timothy Childs. "It's the grape varietal, the terroir, the fermentation, and the distillation all coming together to give a distinctive flavor experience." That's what attracted him to pisco; as a "supertaster," Childs found in pisco a distinctive spirit that pushed his flavor skills in new directions. "That's what gets me excited about pisco," he says.

Here he breaks it down for us, describing the primary characteristics of each of the eight pisco grapes and acholado. Except for Mollar and Uvina, Childs performed this tasting in San Francisco using piscos from ORO, the first brand available in the US offering such a broad line of pisco varietals. (ORO does not make an Uvina or sell Mollar; their tasting notes were provided by Lucero Villagarcia de Bedoya).

Lots more recipes available at www.thepiscobook.com.

* Flavor notes of any acholado vary depending on the constituent ingredients (you can use any mixture of pisco puros). And while most acholados are blends of both aromatic and non-aromatic grapes, not all of them are.

Image source: ClearGrape LLC

A NOTE ABOUT LIMES

When doña Juanita calls the lime the brother of pisco, she's talking about *Citrus aurantifolia*, a lime native to Southeast Asia that was introduced via the Middle East and North Africa to Spain during Moorish times. The Spaniards then brought this lime, with its small spherical fruits, to the New World, where it developed different characteristics in response to the terroir in each of its new lands. The Peruvian lime, brother of pisco, is one of these.

The lime most widely available in the United States is the so-called "Persian" lime, a seedless variety of *Citrus latifolia* that was first bred in California in 1895. It's the fruit that looks like a small green lemon you find in supermarkets everywhere.

The two are not the same. With one or two exceptions (most notably the historical Pisco Punch recipe), "Persian" limes should never be used in pisco drinks (or any drinks from Latin America, from Margaritas to Daiquiris to Caipirhiñas). They are simply the wrong fruit, and impart the wrong flavor.

So do yourself and your guests a favor and track down the right limes. In the United States you're looking for "Key" limes. Usually grown in Mexico, these are northern versions of the limes the Spaniards brought to the Americas. They are close enough in flavor to Peruvian limes to mix beautifully with the dry fruit flavors and floral aromas of great pisco.

When you're buying Key limes, look for firm fruit with uniform green color and a glossy sheen. Once you get them home, let them ripen until they are blushing yellow, indicating that their flavors have developed. Then, cut them in half and juice them with a lime squeezer or cut them in quarters and squeeze them by hand. Don't try to wring every drop of juice from the limes—pressing too hard brings out a bitter note from the rind. Instead, try to get about 80 percent of the juice from each lime: that's the good stuff.

OPPOSITE: Key lime at left, Persian lime at right

Pisco Drink Recipes

If you're experimenting with pisco for the first time, get into the groove with **The Classics** from Peru. Then try some of the **Reinvented Classics**—cocktails you know and love with a pisco twist. **Novo-Andino** and **New American** cocktails will give you a sense of what the mixologists most experienced with pisco are doing these days. And the **Macerados** are a portal into another world entirely.

These 50 recipes are just the start — visit *ThePiscoBook.com*, where you'll find many more and have a chance to contribute your own to share with pisco lovers worldwide. Join us!

THE CLASSICS

DUNCAN NICOL'S PISCO PUNCH · **SIMPLIFIED PISCO PUNCH** · PISCO SOUR · **OLD SCHOOL PISCO SOUR** · CAPITÁN · **PISCOLA** · CHILCANO · **ALGARROBINA**

Duncan Nicol's Pisco Punch

This is the result of Guillermo Toro-Lira's sleuthing to uncover the secrets of the famous pre-Prohibition Pisco Punch served by Duncan Nicol at the Bank Exchange. We have omitted just one ingredient...

INGREDIENTS

PISCO ITALIA
1 FRESH RIPE PINEAPPLE
WATER
PERSIAN LIMES
GOMME SYRUP

PREPARATION

Peel the pineapple and soak the rind in 26 oz of water for 24 hours. Strain and reserve the rind water.

Cut the pineapple's flesh into slices 3/4 inch thick. Remove the core and cut each slice into 3/4 inch squares, reserving the juice. Place the cubes in a tray and puncture each one a few times with a toothpick or a fork, being sure to not poke all the way through. Sprinkle the cubes with pisco Italia, trying to fill the holes. After three hours, strain the pineapple pieces and reserve the juice.

Place the cubes in a glass or ceramic bowl and cover with gomme syrup. Let stand 24 hours, stirring occasionally, then separate the marinated pineapple from the liquid. Add the reserved juices to the liquid—this is now pineapple gomme.

To make punch, stir together 4 parts pisco Italia with 2 parts pineapple gomme, 1 part rind water, and 1 part Persian lime juice. (For a single serving, it's 2 oz pisco Italia, 1 oz pineapple gomme, 1/2 oz rind water, and 1/2 oz Persian lime juice.) Adjust sweet and sour to taste with pineapple gomme and Persian lime juice.

Serve 4 ounces of punch in an 8 ounce glass filled with cracked ice. Garnish with a cube of marinated pineapple.

Guillermo Toro-Lira, Pisco Latin Lounge, San Francisco

Simplified Pisco Punch

Because sometimes you just don't have a day and a half to make a cocktail. Visit thepiscobook.com for more punches.

INGREDIENTS

2 oz PISCO ITALIA OR ACHOLADO
1 oz PINEAPPLE GOMME
1 oz FRESH LIME JUICE
¼ oz ORANGE LIQUEUR
SPLASH GINGER ALE OR GINGER BEER
LIME, LEMON, ORANGE SLICES, PINEAPPLE

PREPARATION

Shake all the ingredients vigorously in a cocktail shaker with plenty of ice for about eight seconds. Then add some more ice, filling up to the edge of the glass. Pour into a 16 oz burgundy glass, garnish with a lime, orange and a lemon wedge inside the glass, and chunks of pineapple on the top of the glass.

Duggan McDonnell, Encanto de Campo Pisco, Cantina, San Francisco

Pisco Sour

This is Peru's National Cocktail (really—it's official; it is served by law at all Peruvian diplomatic functions all over the world). This is the classic recipe you'll find all over the country.

INGREDIENTS

2 oz PISCO QUEBRANTA
½ oz LIME JUICE
½ oz SIMPLE SYRUP
½ EGG WHITE
1 OR 2 DROPS ANGOSTURA BITTERS

PREPARATION

Place pisco, lime juice, simple syrup, egg white and ice in a shaker with six ice cubes and shake it like you mean it. (Alternatively, you can use a blender to whip the drink to classic frothy goodness.) Strain into a short glass and place drops of bitters on top of the foam—the idea is to smell the aromas of the bitters while drinking the Pisco Sour.

Comisión Nacional de Pisco (CONAPISCO)

Old School Pisco Sour

This is the Pisco Sour as prepared at the Bar Inglés at the Hotel Country Club in Lima, using a recipe handed down directly from Victor Morris and Mario Bruiget. "This is the traditional recipe," says Roberto Melendez de la Cruz, "before the cocktail got sweeter and became like a candy in which you couldn't taste the pisco any more."

INGREDIENTS

4 oz PISCO QUEBRANTA
1 oz LIME JUICE
1 oz SIMPLE SYRUP
¼ OF AN EGG WHITE
BITTERS (ANGOSTURA OR PERUVIAN AMARGO)

PREPARATION

Put all the ingredients in a cocktail shaker with ice, shake vigorously for eight to ten seconds, and strain into a chilled keno glass. Place three drops of bitters on top of the foam.

Roberto Melendez de la Cruz, Bar Inglés, Lima

Capitán

Probably originating at the Cocktail Lounge of Lima's Gran Hotel Bolívar in the 1920s, the Capitán is traditionally a warming winter tipple. Historically proportions vary, so try this basic recipe and then adjust it to your taste.

INGREDIENTS

2 oz NON-AROMATIC PISCO
2 oz NOT-TOO-SWEET RED VERMOUTH
   (CINZANO ROSSO)

PREPARATION

Traditionally served in a shot glass at room temperature without any garnish. These days, most people treat the Capitán more like a Manhattan, shaken or (preferably) stirred with ice and served up in a martini glass.

Garnish with a maraschino cherry or, for a more savory drink, an olive or a cocktail onion (which makes the drink a Capitán Inglés).

José Antonio "Chafi" Schiaffino, Malabar, Lima

Piscola

INGREDIENTS

4 oz PISCO
8 oz COLA

PREPARATION

Pour over ice into a highball glass, stir and garnish with a slice of lime.

Chilcano/Cuzco Mule

This classic highball was created by Italian immigrants to Peru in the 1880s, and is a ubiquitous cocktail at hip spots in Lima today, thanks to Omar Cosio's relentless Chilcano evangelism.

INGREDIENTS

2 oz PISCO QUEBRANTA
½ oz FRESH LIME JUICE
GINGER ALE OR GINGER BEER
3 DROPS BITTERS

PREPARATION

Mix pisco and lime juice in a highball glass, fill with ice, top off with ginger ale, stir. Drop the bitters on top and garnish with a lime slice.

Omar Cosio, Viñas de Oro, Lima

Algarrobina

This is a classic ladies' drink, and evokes the ancient tradition of milk-based pisco cocktails. Algarrobina is a syrup made from the seeds of the South American carob (a relative of the Huarango, and different from the Old World carob). If you can't find it, try carob or chocolate syrup. And if you're not into the egg yolk, try coconut crème instead.

INGREDIENTS

2 oz PISCO QUEBRANTA
2 oz EVAPORATED MILK
1 oz SIMPLE SYRUP OR WHITE SUGAR
1 oz ALGARROBINA SYRUP
1 EGG YOLK
7 OR 8 ICE CUBES

PREPARATION

Put everything in a blender and blend until smooth. Pour into a wine glass and sprinkle with ground cinnamon.

Juanita Martínez de Gonzales, Tres Generaciones, Ica

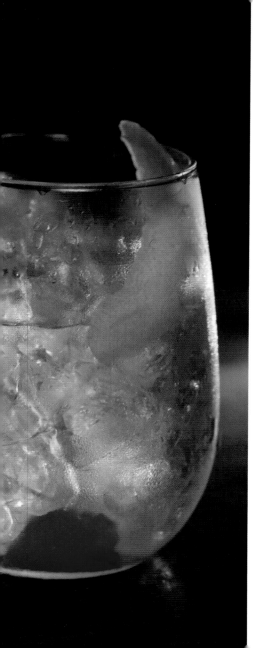

REINVENTED CLASSICS

OLD FASHIONED OR "VIEJO" · **TORONTEL MOJITO** · BLOODY MARY · **PISCO COLLINS**

Old Fashioned or "Viejo"

INGREDIENTS
½ TEASPOON GRANULATED SUGAR OR A
   SUGAR CUBE
3 DASHES ORANGE BITTERS
SPLASH OF WATER
2 oz NON-AROMATIC PISCO
1 PISCO-MACERATED CHERRY (BRANDIED
   CHERRIES WOULD WORK, OR EVEN REAL
   MARASCHINOS)
1 STRIP OF LEMON PEEL
ICE

PREPARATION
Place the sugar in an Old Fashioned glass, and add the bitters, the cherry and a few drops of the cherry liquid, and a small splash of water. Muddle the mixture, and turn the glass so it coats the sides. Twist the lemon peel over the glass, rub it on the rim, and drop it in.

Add the pisco, stir, and add one large piece of ice (or two regular cubes if that is all you have).

Greg Dicum, The Pisco Book, San Francisco

Torontel Mojito

INGREDIENTS
2 oz PISCO TORONTEL
JUICE OF ONE LIME
LEAVES FROM 2 SPRIGS OF MINT
½ oz SIMPLE SYRUP
4 oz SODA WATER

PREPARATION
In a highball glass, muddle the mint leaves in the pisco. Add lime juice, simple syrup, and soda water, stir gently, add ice, and garnish with a sprig of mint.

Greg Dicum, The Pisco Book, San Francisco

Bloody Mary

INGREDIENTS
2 oz PISCO
4 oz TOMATO JUICE
½ TEASPOON FRESHLY GRATED
   HORSERADISH (OPTIONAL)
2 TO 3 DASHES OF WORCESTERSHIRE
   SAUCE
3 DASHES OF TABASCO SAUCE
PINCH OF COARSE SALT
PINCH OF FRESHLY GROUND PEPPER
¼ oz FRESH LEMON OR LIME JUICE
PINCH OF CELERY SALT OR SEEDS, CRUSHED
WEDGES OF LEMON AND LIME

PREPARATION
Combine ingredients in a cocktail shaker over ice, and shake. Strain into a highball glass filled with fresh ice. Garnish with a wedge each of lemon and lime. Optional garnishes include celery, olives, or pickled vegetables.

Pisco Collins

INGREDIENTS
2 oz PISCO
1 oz LEMON OR LIME JUICE
1 TEASPOON SUPERFINE SUGAR
3 oz CLUB SODA
1 REAL MARASCHINO CHERRY
1 ORANGE SLICE

PREPARATION
In a shaker half-filled with ice cubes, combine the pisco, lemon juice, and sugar. Shake well. Strain into a collins glass almost filled with ice cubes. Add the club soda. Stir and garnish with the cherry and the orange slice.

NOVO-ANDINO (NEW-ANDEAN)

NAKED DOG · **MARACUYÁ SOUR** · CHOLOPOLITAN · **GUENASO** · BLACKBERRY PISCOTINI · **APPLE CHILCANITO** · KEY LIME PISCO · **MÉNAGE À TROIS** · MARTINI LIMA 27 · **PASSION FRUIT MARTINI** · MUJERIEGO · **ULTIMATE MARGARITA** · TUMBAO · **STRAWBERRY SOUR**

Naked Dog

The Peruvian Hairless Dog was bred over 1,200 years ago. Pink like this drink, the lively little critters have enjoyed a resurgence lately, as with so much else in Peru.

INGREDIENTS
2 oz PISCO ITALIA
4 oz FRESH PINK GRAPEFRUIT JUICE
GRENADINE

PREPARATION
Pour the ingredients directly into a highball glass full of ice. Stir gently and garnish with a slice of pink grapefruit splashed with a few drops of grenadine.

Hans Hilburg, Living in Peru, Cuzco

Maracuyá Sour

INGREDIENTS
2 oz PISCO QUEBRANTA
1 oz PASSION FRUIT (MARACUYÁ) JUICE
1 oz SIMPLE SYRUP
½ oz FRESH LIME JUICE
½ EGG WHITE
BITTERS

PREPARATION
Prepare as a Pisco Sour: put pisco, juices, simple syrup, egg white, and ice in a shaker and shake hard or use a blender. Strain into a short glass and garnish with a lime wedge. Drop three drops of bitters on top of the froth.

Juanita Martínez de Gonzales, Tres Generaciones, Ica

Cholopolitan

INGREDIENTS
3 oz PISCO ACHOLADO
3 oz CRANBERRY JUICE
¼ oz LIME JUICE
¼ oz ORANGE LIQUEUR
½ oz PASSION FRUIT JUICE

PREPARATION
Pour all ingredients into a shaker, shake, and strain into a chilled martini glass. Garnish with a curled lime peel.

Hans Hilburg, Living in Peru, Cuzco

Guenaso

Guenaso means awesome, better than great, and that's exactly how this cocktail tastes.

INGREDIENTS
2 oz PISCO QUEBRANTA
5 BASIL LEAVES
½ PERSIAN LIME
1 oz PASSION FRUIT JUICE
1 oz GOMME SYRUP
SODA WATER

PREPARATION
Place the lime, broken up basil leaves, and gum syrup in a shaker, muddle once and add pisco, passion fruit juice, and six ice cubes. Shake for six seconds. Serve in a 12 oz glass, adding ice, a basil leaf, and a half moon of lime.

Raúl Rosas Sayas, Astrid & Gastón, Lima

Blackberry Piscotini

INGREDIENTS
2 oz PISCO ITALIA
2 ½ oz BLACKBERRY OR MULBERRY JUICE
¾ oz SIMPLE SYRUP
½ oz CRÈME DE CASSIS

PREPARATION
Pour into a shaker filled with ice, shake, and strain into a 10 oz chilled martini glass.
You can substitute virtually any berry juice. Try raspberry juice with Chambord instead of Crème de Cassis.

Enrique Vidarte Morales, Cala, Lima

Apple Chilcanito

INGREDIENTS
2 oz PISCO ITALIA
¼ oz APPLE LIQUEUR
½ GREEN APPLE
3 oz GINGER ALE

PREPARATION
Blend all the ingredients except the ginger ale in a blender for approximately 15 seconds. Strain and serve directly into a collins glass with a lot of ice. Stir in the ginger ale. Garnish with a lime wedge and and apple slice.

Hans Hilburg, Living in Peru, Cuzco

Key Lime Pisco

INGREDIENTS
1 oz PISCO QUEBRANTA
1 oz GRANULATED SUGAR
¾ oz CONDENSED MILK
¾ oz FRESH SQUEEZED LIME JUICE
1 oz ICE

PREPARATION
In a blender, blend ice, sugar, lime juice, condensed milk, and 1/4 of the pisco until stiff. Mound into a Margarita glass, and pour a moat of the rest of the pisco around it. Garnish with a round of lime.

Enrique Vidarte Morales, Cala, Lima

Ménage à Trois

Guillermo calls this a Ménage à Trois because it is a grape three-way: pisco, champagne, and whole grapes.

INGREDIENTS
1 ½ oz PISCO
2 oz CHAMPAGNE OR SPANISH CAVA
½ oz SIMPLE SYRUP
¾ oz LIME JUICE
8 SEEDLESS GREEN TABLE GRAPES

PREPARATION
In an Old Fashioned glass, crush 6-8 grapes, fill the glass with crushed ice, pour in the other ingredients, and stir.

You can also turn this into a Peruvian 75— just substitute lemon for lime, hold back on the syrup a bit, leave out the grapes, and garnish with a pisco macerated cherry or maraschino cherry.

Guillermo Ferreyros, Pisco 100, Lima

Martini Lima 27

INGREDIENTS
2 oz PISCO ITALIA
3 oz PEACH JUICE (FRESH PUREED PEACHES
    OR PEACH NECTAR)
BERRY SYRUP (STRAWBERRIES,
    BLUEBERRIES, BLACKBERRIES, ETC.)

PREPARATION
Pour all ingredients into a shaker, shake, and
strain into a chilled martini glass. Drizzle berry
syrup on top.

Jesús Ávila Sovero, Malabar, Lima

Passion Fruit Martini

INGREDIENTS
2½ oz PISCO
¼ oz ORANGE LIQUEUR
3 oz PASSION FRUIT JUICE
5 ICE CUBES
1 REAL MARASCHINO CHERRY

PREPARATION
Pour all ingredients into a shaker, shake, and
strain into a chilled Martini glass. Garnish with
the cherry.

Hans Hilburg, Living in Peru, Cuzco

Mujeriego

Mujeriego means "Ladies' Man" or even "Player."

INGREDIENTS
3 oz PISCO ACHOLADO
½ oz LIME JUICE
½ oz GOMME SYRUP
3½ oz ITALIA OR MUSCAT GRAPE JUICE

PREPARATION
Mix ingredients in a cocktail shaker, add ice,
and shake. Strain into highball glass filled with
ice. Finish off with soda water.

Jaime Pesaque Roose, Mayta, Lima

Ultimate Margarita

INGREDIENTS

1 oz PISCO MOSTO VERDE
½ oz COINTREAU
½ oz GRAND MARNIER
¾ oz FRESH LIME JUICE
¾ oz FRESH LEMON JUICE
1½ oz SIMPLE SYRUP

PREPARATION

Fill shaker 2/3 full with cubed ice. Add ingredients and shake. Strain into a glass filled with ice and garnish with lime and orange wedges.

Johnny Schuler, Pisco Portón, Lima

Tumbao

Tumbao is Limeño slang for a great dancer. We like to call this one "Hot Pants."

INGREDIENTS

2 oz PISCO ITALIA
½ oz MELON LIQUEUR
½ oz ORANGE LIQUEUR
2 oz ORANGE JUICE
2 oz PINEAPPLE JUICE

PREPARATION

Mix ingredients in a cocktail shaker, add ice, and shake. Strain into a chilled Martini glass, then shake your tail feathers.

Jaime Pesaque Roose, Mayta, Lima

Strawberry Sour

INGREDIENTS

2 oz PISCO MOSTO VERDE
1½ oz CRUSHED STRAWBERRIES
½ oz FRESH LIME JUICE
1 oz SIMPLE SYRUP

PREPARATION

Fill shaker 2/3 full with cubed ice, add ingredients, shake, and strain into a chilled glass. Garnish with a strawberry.

Johnny Schuler, Pisco Portón, Lima

NEW AMERICAN

FLOR DE LIMA · **SCARLET FIRE** · FALLEN ANGEL · **PERUVIAN SPARKLE** · THE ROYAL PERUVIAN SIDECAR · **PERUVIAN PATADA** · STRAWBERRY PISCO COLLINS OR GIMLET · **PEACH GINGER PISCO SOUR** · YERBA MATÉ PISCO PUNCH · **ORANGE FLYER** · FIRECRACKER COCKTAIL · **SPARKLING RUBY** · SAXON · **IMPROVED MARTINEZ**

Flor de Lima

INGREDIENTS
1½ oz PISCO TORONTEL
¾ oz ELDERFLOWER LIQUEUR
  (ST. GERMAIN)
1 oz ORANGE JUICE
½ oz FRESH LIME JUICE
¼ oz SIMPLE SYRUP

PREPARATION
Pour all the ingredients over ice, shake, and strain into a chilled Martini glass. Garnish with an orange twist.

Sandra Manhart, Fresca, San Francisco

Scarlet Fire

INGREDIENTS
2 oz PISCO ACHOLADO
2 oz PASSION FRUIT JUICE
2-4 BAR SPOONS PRICKLY PEAR SORBET
  (CIAO BELLA)
¼ oz GINGER LIQUEUR
½ oz FRESH LIME JUICE
2 MINT LEAVES

PREPARATION
Hand spank the mint and combine with all the ingredients, except the sparkling water, in an ice-filled shaker. Shake enough to dissolve the sorbet. Pour into a coupe or sour glass. Garnish with freshly spanked mint.

Timothy Childs, ClearGrape, San Francisco

 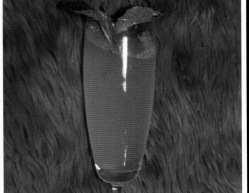 

Fallen Angel

INGREDIENTS
2 oz PISCO ACHOLADO
½ oz APEROL
¾ oz LEMON JUICE
½ oz EGG WHITE
BAR/SPOON OF RASPBERRY JAM
DASH SIMPLE SYRUP

PREPARATION
Combine all ingredients and shake vigorously with no ice for 10 to 15 seconds. Add ice and shake vigorously until the drink takes on a voluptuous creamy texture. Strain into a chilled coupe and garnish with one raspberry.

Erick Castro, Rickhouse, San Francisco

Peruvian Sparkle

INGREDIENTS
½ oz PISCO MOSCATEL
DASH MELON LIQUEUR
DASH ORANGE LIQUEUR
½ oz PINEAPPLE JUICE
CHAMPAGNE, CAVA, OR SPARKLING WHITE WINE

PREPARATION
Shake all ingredients, except the champagne, and strain into a champagne glass. Top off with sparkling white wine and garnish with mint sprig.

Sandra Manhart, Fresca, San Francisco

The Royal Peruvian Sidecar

INGREDIENTS
2 oz PISCO NEGRA CRIOLLA
¾ oz ROYAL COMBIER LIQUEUR
4 HONEY-SOAKED LEMON WHEELS
½ oz LEMON JUICE
ORANGE ZEST FOR RIM
½ oz HONEY TO MAKE RIM STICKY

PREPARATION
Muddle 4 honey-soaked lemon wheels. Add all ingredients except orange zest and honey. Shake and double strain ingredients into a coupe glass rimmed with honey and orange zest.

Shane McKnight, Best Beverage Catering, San Francisco

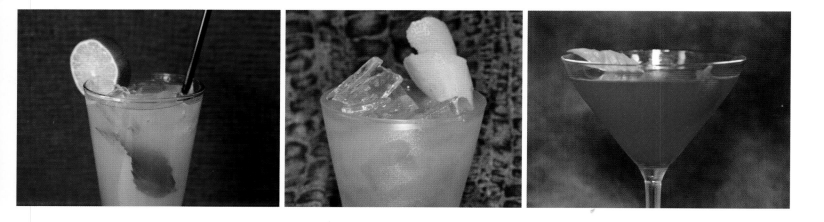

Peruvian Patada

Patada means "kick" in Spanish.

INGREDIENTS
1½ oz PISCO QUEBRANTA
½ oz CANTON GINGER LIQUEUR
1 oz GINGER BEER
1 oz LIME JUICE
¼ oz SIMPLE SYRUP
10 MINT LEAVES

PREPARATION
Muddle mint, lime, and syrup. Add spirits and ice, shake, and strain over fresh ice, and top off with ginger beer. Garnish with a mint sprig.

James Schenk, Destino and Pisco Latin Lounge, San Francisco

Presidio Punch

INGREDIENTS
2 oz PISCO ACHOLADO
1½ oz POM WONDERFUL MANGO
1 oz MIGHTY TEA LEAF CHAMOMILE
   TEA SYRUP
½ oz LEMON JUICE

PREPARATION
Make a tea syrup by steeping one bag of tea in 8 oz hot water, then mixing it in a 1:1 ratio with cane sugar.

In a mixing glass, add all ingredients, fill with ice, and shake for 10 seconds. Strain over ice and garnish with a wide lemon twist.

H. Joseph Ehrmann, Elixir Bar, San Francisco

Strawberry Pisco Collins or Gimlet

INGREDIENTS
2 oz TORONTEL
2 MUDDLED STRAWBERRIES
5 BASIL LEAVES
¾ oz LIME JUICE
¾ oz AGAVE NECTAR

PREPARATION
Muddle basil and add all ingredients to a cocktail shaker. Shake and double strain into Martini glass for a Gimlet, or shake and strain into a collins glass over ice with a splash of soda for a Collins. Garnish with a basil leaf.

Shane McKnight, Best Beverage Catering, San Francisco

Yerba Mate Pisco Punch

INGREDIENTS

2 oz PISCO ACHOLADO
½ oz ORANGE LIQUEUR (ROYAL COMBIER)
2 oz GUAYAKI ORGANIC LEMON YERBA MATÉ
1 oz GINGER-HONEY SYRUP
1 oz PINEAPPLE JUICE
½ oz FRESH LIME JUICE
4-6 DROPS OF PEYCHAUD'S BITTERS

PREPARATION

Add all ingredients except bitters and ice to a mixing cup, and pour back and forth to another mixing cup. Transfer into a 12 oz tumbler, top with four drops of bitters, and garnish with a mint sprig.

Shane McKnight, Best Beverage Catering, San Francisco

Este Gabacho

INGREDIENTS

2 oz PISCO ACHOLADO
¾ oz DOLIN DRY VERMOUTH
¾ oz DOLIN BIANCO VERMOUTH
2 DASHES OF CITRUS BITTERS (GRAPEFRUIT AND ORANGE)

PREPARATION

Stir all ingredients in a mixing glass with ice. Strain into a cocktail coupe and garnish with zest and twist from a grapefruit.

Ryan McGrale, Flatiron Lounge, New York

Orange Flyer

INGREDIENTS

2 oz PISCO TORONTEL
1 oz SPARKLING LEMON SODA
1 SMALL SCOOP OF BLOOD ORANGE SORBET (CIAO BELLA)

PREPARATION

Add sorbet and pisco to a shaker glass. Shake until sorbet is fully dissolved. Pour into a martini glass and top with chilled lemon soda. Garnish with a sprig of mint.

Janis Nakano Spivack, ClearGrape, San Francisco.

Firecracker Cocktail

INGREDIENTS

1½ oz PISCO TORONTEL
½ oz CREMA DE MEZCAL (DEL MAGUEY)
½ oz AGAVE NECTAR
½ oz FRESH SQUEEZED LIME JUICE
1 oz PINEAPPLE JUICE
½ oz ST. ELIZABETH ALLSPICE DRAM
CINNAMON SUGAR RIM

PREPARATION

Combine Mezcal and agave nectar, and stir until all the agave has dissolved.

Grind fresh cinnamon into sugar bowl, mix with sugar. With a lemon wedge, wet the rim of a cocktail glass, and apply a thin layer of cinnamon sugar onto the rim. Place the glass into the freezer to harden.

Pour all liquid ingredients into a shaker, add ice, and shake vigorously for seven or eight seconds. Strain into the prepared cocktail glass and serve.

Dushan Zaric, Employees Only, New York

Sparkling Ruby

INGREDIENTS

1½ oz PISCO
½ oz APEROL
2 oz RUBY RED GRAPEFRUIT JUICE
DRY SPARKLING WINE

PREPARATION

Chill all ingredients and build in a flute in the order listed. Garnish with lemon zest.

Meryll Cawn, Wine Think Tank,
Kentfield Marketing Group, San Francisco.

Saxon

INGREDIENTS

1½ oz PISCO ACHOLADO
½ oz YELLOW CHARTREUSE
¾ oz SIMPLE SYRUP
1 oz LEMON JUICE
4 BASIL LEAVES
1 ORANGE PEEL
2 DASHES BITTERS

PREPARATION

Place two dashes of bitters in a bucket glass filled with ice. Pour all ingredients into a shaker and shake. Double strain into the glass, and garnish with basil and an orange twist.

Enrique Sanchez, La Mar, San Francisco

Improved Martinez

INGREDIENTS

1½ oz PISCO TORONTEL OR ACHOLADO
½ oz DRY VERMOUTH
¼ oz MARASCHINO LIQUEUR
¼ oz YELLOW CHARTREUSE
2 DASHES ORANGE BITTERS

PREPARATION

Slowly stir all the ingredients 40 times with ice, strain into a cocktail coupe. Garnish with a fat lemon peel.

Duggan McDonnell, Encanto de Campo Pisco,
Cantina, San Francisco

MACERADOS

MACERADO DE COCA · **MACERADO DE GUINDA (WILD CHERRY)** · MACERADO DE KIÓN (GINGER) · **MACERADO DE HIERBA LUISA (LEMONGRASS)** · MACERADO DE MANZANILLA (CHAMOMILE) · **BEE'S SIP** · MAYTINI · **THE GINGER** · THE LEMONGRASS

Macerados are piscos that have been infused with fruits or herbs. They can be extremely traditional—a macerado of raisins is traditionally drunk straight up on cold winter nights in Ica, and macerados of coca have long fueled all night revelries in Peru.

Making macerados is not simply a matter of dumping a bunch of flavorings into some pisco and leaving them there. Rather, each ingredient is different, and requires different lengths of time in the pisco.

Here are some macerados, and some recipes that use them to great effect, from some of the most inventive yet traditional mixologists working in the world today.

Macerado de Coca

INGREDIENTS
9 oz COCA LEAVES
34 oz PISCO QUEBRANTA
8 oz SIMPLE SYRUP

PREPARATION
Mix all the ingredients in a glass container big enough so the leaves float freely and aren't compressed. After a week, taste the macerado and adjust it to taste (sometimes doña Juanita adds Huarango honey). Let the macerado age for a month before using.

Juanita Martínez de Gonzales,
Tres Generaciones, Ica

Macerado de Guinda (wild cherry)

INGREDIENTS

1 PINT OF PISCO QUEBRANTA
1 CUP OF CHERRIES

PREPARATION

Pit the cherries, and put them and their pits in the pisco. Let sit for two months.

Greg Dicum, The Pisco Book

Macerado de Kión (ginger)

INGREDIENTS

1 LITER PISCO QUEBRANTA
2 oz FRESH GINGER

PREPARATION

Peel the ginger and slice it thinly. Add it to the pisco and let it sit for a week.

Jaime Pesaque Roose, Mayta, Lima

Macerado de Hierba Luisa (lemongrass)

INGREDIENTS

1 LITER PISCO QUEBRANTA
1 BUNCH FRESH LEMONGRASS

PREPARATION

Put 1/3 of a bunch of lemongrass in the pisco and let it sit for five days. Remove the lemongrass and replace with another 1/3 of a bunch for five more days. Then remove that lemongrass and add the final 1/3 of the bunch for five more days.

Jaime Pesaque Roose, Mayta, Lima

Macerado de Manzanilla (Chamomile)

INGREDIENTS

1 750 ML BOTTLE OF PISCO
½ oz CHAMOMILE TEA FLOWERS

PREPARATION

Infuse for 15 minutes, then fine strain.

James Meehan, PDT, New York

The Lemongrass

INGREDIENTS
2 oz PISCO MACERATED WITH LEMONGRASS
4 DROPS OF BITTERS
¼ oz FRESH LIME JUICE
4-5 oz GINGER ALE
ICE

PREPARATION
Pour pisco and lime juice in shaker, shake, and strain over fresh ice. Add ginger ale and top with bitters. Serve in a highball or collins glass.

Note: To make **The Ginger** cocktail, follow these same instructions only replacing 2 oz Pisco macerated with Ginger instead of lemongrass.

Jaime Pesaque Roose, Mayta, Lima.

Maytini

INGREDIENTS
1½ oz PISCO QUEBRANTA
1 oz PISCO MACERATED WITH GINGER
½ oz GOMME SYRUP
3½ oz UNSWEETENED PASSION FRUIT
   PUREE

PREPARATION

Pour all ingredients into a shaker, shake, and strain into a chilled Martini glass.

Jaime Pesaque Roose, Mayta, Lima

Bee's Sip

INGREDIENTS
2½ oz PISCO MACERATED WITH CHAMOMILE
1 oz JUNMAI SAKE (MASUMI "OKUDEN")
½ oz HONEY LIQUEUR (BÄRENJÄGER)
ELDERFLOWER LIQUEUR (ST. GERMAIN)

PREPARATION
Mix ingredients and stir with ice. Strain into a chilled coupe that has been rinsed with St. Germain. Garnish with a lemon twist.

James Meehan, PDT, New York

Glossary

ACHOLADO pisco that is a blend of different grapes, usually including both aromatic and non-aromatic grapes

AGUARDIENTE the generic term for any distilled liquor

ALBILLA one of the aromatic grape varieties

ALEMBIQUE a copper pot still with a "gooseneck" that purifies the distillate somewhat

ALGARROBINA a syrup made from carob or huarango beans; also a cocktail that uses this syrup

BODEGA a place where wine or pisco is made

BODY the main part of a still run

BOTIJA a distinctive clay vessel used in the past for fermentation and storage

CAPITÁN a classic pisco cocktail made with sweet vermouth

CHICHARRÓN aguardiente fresh from the still; it requires at least three months rest to be pisco

CHILCANO a classic pisco cocktail made with ginger ale

FALCA a primitive pot still

GALERA a method of growing grapes in which the vines are tall, allowing workers to walk in their shade

HEAD the first part of a still run, containing more volatile alcohols and other compounds. It is noxious, and is discarded

HUARANGO a leguminous tree native to the Peruvian desert; its wood is hard and dense, and the huge trees can be very old; cutting these endangered trees is now forbidden

ITALIA the most popular of the aromatic grape varieities

LA VENDÍMIA harvest, also a big grape harvest festival held each March in Ica

LAS ONCE a traditional tipple taken in late morning, often consisting of a shot of pisco and a few olives

MACERADO pisco that has been infused with herbs, fruits, or spices

MOLLAR one of the non-aromatic pisco grapes

MOSCATEL one of the aromatic pisco grapes; also called Muscat in France and Moscato Rosso in Italy

MOSTO the "must" of juice after grapes are pressed. Unlike "must" in North American winemaking, in Peru, "mosto" never has skins, seeds, or stems in it, and for that reason we use it as a separate term in this book

MOSTO VERDE mosto that has not been completely fermented, or pisco distilled from mosto that has not been completely fermented

MOSTO YEMA pisco made only from juice pressed manually from the grapes, as in cuvées

NEGRA CORRIENTE another name for the non–aromatic grape Negra Criolla

NEGRA CRIOLLA the original pisco grape brought from Spain; also known as Mission Black in California

PISCO a mixable white spirit distilled from grapes in Peru

PISCO SOUR traditional pisco cocktail, and Peru's national cocktail

PURO pisco made from a single grape variety; also a drink of pure pisco with nothing added to it

QUEBRANTA one of the nonaromatic grape varieties, and the most widely used pisco grape

TAIL the end of a still run; it contains fusel oils and other heavier compounds and is discarded

TINAJA a big clay urn used in the old days for fermentation, resting, and storage of pisco

TORONTEL one of the aromatic grape varieties, known as Frontingan in France and Moscato Bianco in Italy

UVINA a non–aromatic grape variety, and the least-used pisco grape; its use in pisco is allowed only in one valley

Index

acholado 25
Acurio, Gastón 70, 89, 100
aging 39
alembique 31, 36-37
Algarrobina 64
Amoretti, Jesús 31, 79
Association of Independent Pisco Tasters 82
Atahualpa 17
Ayahuasca (bar) 85

Bank Exchange 47-51
Bar Inglés 55, 89-91
Barsol 95, 102
Biondi 70, 79
bitters 53
botijas 21, 28
Brescia Group 78
Bruiget, Mario 53

Cala 89
Campo de Encanto 99
Capitán, origins 54
ceviche 70
chicha 59
chicharrón 39, 79
Chilcano 64, 85
Chilcano, origins 44
Childs, Timothy 99-100

cinchona 53
ClearGrape 100
cocaine (in cocktails) 97-98
Cosio, Omar 85

da Trindade-Asher, Melanie and Lizzie 95-96
Denomination of Origin 72-73, 81-82
Denomination of Origin, cheating 82
Denomination of Origin, Chilean 54

el corte 64

falca 34, 36-37
fermentation 37
Ferreyros, Guillermo 98

galera system 21
Gran Hotel Bolívar 54
grape intensity 36
grape varieties and flavors 106-107
grapes, aromatic 12, 43
grapes, negra corriente 25
grapes, negra criollo 23
grapes, non-aromatic 12
grapes, origins 23
grapes, Moscatel 43
grapes, Quebranta 25, 39, 81
guano 43

hangover, impossibility with pisco 102
Hotel Country Club 55
Hotel Maury 53, 55
House of Pisco 99
huarango 22
Huaringas Bar 85

Ica Valley, terroir 77
Ica, founding 19
immigration, Italian 44
INDECOPI 82
Italia 43, 94
Italia, availability in the US 100

jaranas 60-61

Kipling, Rudyard 48

La Caravedo 76, 103
Land Reform 57
las once 28, 63
Ledesma, Cecila 73, 78
Lima, cafés 63
limes 109
Lloret de Mola, Diego 95, 100

Macchu Pisco 96
macerados 61, 64, 86
Malabar 86

Marroquín, Soledad 84
Martínez, Juanita 33, 64, 80
Mayta 86
McDonnell, Duggan 99
Mejía, Rodolfo 27, 63-64
Melendez, Roberto 89
Montgomery Block 47
Morris' Bar 52-53
Morris, Victor 52-53, 94-95
Moscatel *see grapes*
mosto verde 12
mosto, definition 22

Nazca Lines 17
Nicol, Duncan 51, 94
novo-Andino cuisine 70

ORO 100

Peru, geography 17
Peru, independence 41
Peruvian bark 53
Pesaque, Jaime 86
Peschiera, Rodrigo 74-77
phylloxera 44
Pisco (town) 19
pisco aromatizado 65
pisco Italia *see Italia*
Pisco Latin Lounge 96
Pisco Portón 102-103
Pisco Punch 51
Pisco Punch, lost recipe 94-95, 96-97

Pisco Punch, secret ingredient 97
pisco puro 25
Pisco Sour 57
Pisco Sour Day 67
Pisco Sour, best in Lima 89-91
Pisco Sour, dominance 67
Pisco Sour, origins 52-53
Pisco Sour, variations 85
Pisco Sour, vs Chilcano 85
pisco, Chilean 54, 93
pisco, definition 12, 73
pisco, earliest evidence 21
pisco, earliest use of name 41
pisco, pronunciation 11
pisco-making, modern 74, 80
pisco-making, traditional 22
Pizzaro, Francisco 17-18
Polis, Ricardo 79, 84
prices 82
production 82
Prohibition 51
Punch 51

Qollqe 73, 78
quality 82
quebranta *see grapes*

Romero, Carlos 99

San Francisco 47, 93
Sánchez, Enrique 100
Santiago Quierolo 44, 63, 74, 79

Schenk, James 96, 100
Schiaffino, José Antonio (Chafi) 86
Schuler, Johnny 102
Spanish conquest 17
stomping 28

tasting 82, 105-106
technology 74, 80
Temoche, William 72
tinajas 21
Toro-Lira, Guillermo 52, 93-94, 96, 98, 100
Tres Generactiones 33-39, 64-65, 74, 80
Twain, Mark 48

Vendímia 28, 65-67
Vidarte, Enrique 89
Viejo Tonel 72
Villagarcía, Lucero 82-83
Viñas de Oro 74, 78-81, 85, 100
vines, first in Peru 19

War of the Pacific 43

Further Resources

There are just a handful of good books about pisco out there. In Peru, Mariella Balbi's "Pisco es Peru" and the Interbank book "Pisco — Espíritu de Plata, Esencia del Perú" provide the best grounding in the drink's deep history and cultural impact.

In the United States, the best historical resources bar none are Guillermo Toro-Lira's "Wings of Cherubs" and especially his source book of historical evidence entitled "History of Pisco in San Francisco: A Scrapbook of First Hand Accounts." He also has written a number of important historical papers that can be found at his website piscopunch.com

Because the world of pisco is evolving so rapidly, the best current material is found online—from cultural paeans to exhaustively cataloged tasting notes to the various websites of the best pisco makers. The best place to start is at the regularly updated list of resources found in the online companion to this book: thepiscobook.com

Acknowledgements

HISTORIANS

Guillermo Toro-Lira, José Antonio "Chafi" Schiaffino

BARTENDERS AND RESTAURANTEURS

Cesar Aching, Gastón Acurio, Jesús Ávila Sovero, Augusta Bernales Wiesse, Juilo Calvo-Perez, Erick Castro, Meryll Cawn, Raúl Diez Canseco, H. Joseph Ehrmann, Andrew Generalao, Hans Hilburg, Ryan McGrale, James Meehan, Roberto Melendez de la Cruz, Sandra Manhart, Shane McKnight, Jimi Moran, Diego Oka, Jaime Pesaque Roose, Maria del Rosario Alcorta, Raúl Rosas Sayas, Enrique Sánchez, Rocio Sánchez, James Schenk, Enrique Vidarte Morales, Carlos Yturria, Dushan Zaric

TASTERS

Soledad Marroquín, Livio Pastorino Wagner, Lucero Villagarcía de Bedoya

RECIPE-TASTING TEAM

Shelley Alger, Timothy Childs, Greg Dicum, Duggan McDonnell, Shane McKnight, Shiaosan Williams-Sheng

PISCO-MAKERS AND IMPORTERS

Guillermo Ferreyros, Luís Antonio Gonzales Martinez, Luís Antonio Gonzales Missa, Alfredo Gordillo Andrade, Bertrand Jolly, Cecilia Ledesma, Diego Loret de Mola, Jaime Marimon Pizarro, Juanita Martínez de Gonzales, Rodolfo "La Leyenda" Mejía, Javier Merino, Duggan McDonnell, Walter Moore, Lyris Monasterio, Ricardo Polis, Carlos Romero, Carlos Rotondo Donola, Johnny Schuler, Ronnie Shialer, Davide Solari Berisso, Miguel Solari, Magin Sole, William Temoche Solis, Melanie & Lizzie da Trindade-Asher, Mario Vingerhoets

ALEMBIQUE MAKER

Jesús Amoretti Yataco

AND OTHERS...

Kim Ciabattari, Romy Colombatto, David Corso, Omar Cosio, Olga Gonzales, Tom Ingalls, Nina Luttinger, Kseniya Makarova, Andrew Mariani, Donna and Michael Morris, Ananda Neil, Steve Raye, Kathryn Shedrick, Janis Nakano Spivack, Raúl Vargas, Gregory Willis, Javier Zaragoza, The Pisco Society of San Francisco, and everyone else who has helped out in making this book possible.

The Pisco Book was typeset in Trade Gothic
with display type in Gotham.

Book design by Ingalls Design, San Francisco
Designers: Kim Ciabattari, Tom Ingalls, Kseniya Makarova
and Stephanie Szabo